This fictional story set in a real setting is or
olds in particular will enjoy. The adventures
spend 'a summer holiday which none of th
simply and graphically described. The autho .... the apprehension of
the children as they are obliged by their mother's sudden illness to spend
their break from school with Great-Aunt Eliza (who also is apprehensive)
n her rambling old riverside mansion in rural Dorset. As the story unfolds,
Tilly, Toby, Alfie and their great-aunt bond happily and the old house reveals
secrets which take them and the reader on an exciting and challenging
treasure hunt.

The book is action-packed and provides an easy and captivating read for
children, while adults who pick it up will also find it engaging and moving.
The story is tinged with sadness, and recourse to prayer and renewed faith
feature naturally and sensitively in the narrative. I happily recommend it to
all ages.

Jean Howell, former headmistress

© Day One Publications 2019

First printed 2019

ISBN 978-1-84625-652-3

Published by Day One Publications
Ryelands Road, Leominster, HR6 8NZ

TEL 01568 613 740 FAX 01568 611 473

email—sales@dayone.co.uk

UK web site—www.dayone.co.uk

Designed by **documen**
Cover designed by Kathryn Chedgzoy
Printed by TJ International

Dedication

To my dear friends, Rosemary and David,
and their grandchildren,
Genevieve, Miranda, Eleanor,
Emily, Thomas and Annabel

Acknowledgements

My thanks to:

Rosemary and David, for allowing me to use their home, Greystones, as the location of this story. Although the location is real, the story is entirely fictional, as are all the characters.

My editors and publisher, for their encouragement and help.

Those of my friends who are willing to read my manuscripts and give me their valued comments.

And, as ever, my dear husband, Malcolm, for all his support and encouragement.

Chapter one

It was a hot July afternoon. The sky was bright blue, with just a few very fluffy white clouds drifting across from time to time. Tilly was sitting near the window, and the sun was blazing through the glass, making it hard to concentrate. She gazed out at the school playing field just outside, her mind wandering, daydreaming, thinking of her brothers at primary school who had sports day that day. Both Toby and Alfie were good at running. She hoped they would win some prizes. A smile curved around her mouth as she thought of her mum and dad who loved to take part in the parents' three-legged race, and often won. It would be so lovely to be outside in the sunshine cheering them on, instead of having to listen to Miss Senoire waffling on about French verbs!

Suddenly, she was startled out of her daydream as she heard her teacher address her:

'Mam'zelle Tilly, perhaps you would kindly decline the verb *avoir* for us all, instead of looking out of zee window!' Miss Senoire said in her most severe voice.

Tilly, her face bright red with embarrassment, stood up and began reciting. What a good job she knew her verbs by heart!

When she had finished she sat down and tried to concentrate until the end of the lesson. It was such a relief when the bell rang to announce the end of the school day. Tilly gathered up her books and bag and made for the door. Her friend, Faith, was waiting for her in the cloakroom. They usually walked home together, but today they were going home from Deepvale Academy via the primary school to meet up with their younger siblings and parents, and to join in the fun at the end of the sports day. It was a tradition that those who had left the previous year were welcomed back to have ice cream and to see their former teachers and their friends who had gone to different senior schools.

In spite of the heat, the girls ran as fast as they could, as they were so pleased to be going back to St Martin's Primary.

'I can't believe we've nearly finished year 7 already!' commented Faith breathlessly. 'It wasn't as bad as we thought it might be, was it?'

'Once I managed to find my way around all the buildings, it was fine,' answered Tilly, 'but I still miss St Martin's. I loved it in the summer on days like today when we took our books out and had lessons under the trees. I guess I just love being outdoors—we all do: Dad says we are an "outdoorsy" family. I bet my brothers have won some races today. To think that next term Toby will be coming to Deepvale with us, and so will your sister!'

'It'll be easier for Grace,' replied Faith. 'At least I can show her around. I don't s'pose Toby will want his sister doing that!'

They soon arrived at the junior school where the head teacher was waiting to let them in. But her usually smiling face was looking sad, and she took Tilly's hand and asked her to come into her office. Tilly froze inside— she sensed something was wrong. What had happened?

'Faith, dear,' the head said to her friend, 'your mum and Grace are waiting for you. I just need to have a little chat with Tilly.'

Once they were inside the office, the kind teacher put her arm around Tilly and began to tell her what had happened that afternoon.

'I need you to be very brave,' she explained, 'because you will need to be strong to help Toby, and especially Alfie, as he is only 9. Something very sad happened as your mum and dad were running the three-legged race. I'm afraid that your mum collapsed and has been taken by the air ambulance to Bristol Royal Infirmary.'

Tilly's face went white and she began to feel dizzy as she tried to take in the news.

'Will she be all right?' she whispered. 'She isn't dead, is she? Please tell me she isn't dead!'

'When the paramedics arrived she was very ill, but still alive, and they began to help her at once. We don't know all the details, but it seems she may have had a blood vessel burst and bleed into her brain, and because she was running and tied to your dad, she has broken her leg as well. She is very, very ill, and that is why the air ambulance was called to take her to the best hospital to help her. Your dad is with her, and Alfie and Toby are with Faith's mum. She will look after you until your dad gets back from the hospital. I'm so sorry to bring you such bad news, but we are all praying for your mum to get better. I have phoned the headmaster of Deepvale, so he knows the news and will give you leave from school if you need it.'

The headmistress pressed her buzzer and then the secretary brought in Faith's mum, who took her, Toby and Alfie back to her home, along with Faith and Grace.

Tilly felt numb and cold. Surely it wasn't true? There must be some mistake, she kept telling herself; but deep down inside she knew it was true, and she did have to be brave and help her brothers while they waited for news.

Chapter two

The next few days were very difficult. The time seemed to go so very slowly as the children waited for news of their mum. Each morning, after taking them to school, their dad went to the hospital and sat by their mum's bed, but she was unconscious and covered with all sorts of tubes and wires. After school they went home with Faith and Grace, whose mother cooked them a meal before taking them home later in the evening to stay the night with their dad.

Tilly was worried about him, as well as being terribly worried about her mum. He looked older and his eyes were red from where he had been crying, although he tried to put on a brave face when he was with them. She did all she could to help—washing the dirty clothes and ironing the uniforms for school. It helped her to have lots of things to do: it stopped her thinking about what might happen to their mum. Dad gave them lots of hugs and tried to tell them he was sure their mum would improve, but it could take many months. After an operation to stop the bleeding in her brain, he had been told she would be kept unconscious, giving her brain time to heal.

'I have to make arrangements for you all to go away for the school holidays,' he told them one evening, about a week after the accident. 'I'm going to ask my aunt Eliza if you could possibly stay with her. I know you don't know your great-aunt Eliza very well, but she does live in a big house not far from the sea. It's not too far away, and I can come and see you all sometimes.'

Tilly's face fell. She wanted to stamp her foot and scream that she didn't want to go to Aunt Eliza's house, however nice it was, but she knew that would upset her dad even more. So she just bit her lip and kept the words inside herself. Tilly could remember her great-aunt from the time she had visited them all when their nan had celebrated her eightieth birthday. She had seemed very severe, with her grey hair pulled back into a bun, and she wore dreary clothes, had looked at the boys as if they were little nuisances, and kept on nagging about 'good manners'. (Tilly often thought her brothers were nuisances too, but if anyone else criticized them, that was a different matter!)

Tilly, Toby and Alfie loved their nan—she was such fun, and her face was always full of smiles, but recently she had fallen and broken her hip. Although it was now healing, she was in a care home for a few weeks until she could walk properly and manage to look after herself. They understood that she couldn't look after them while their mum was ill. Neither could their grandma and grandpa, because they lived thousands of miles away in Africa, where Grandpa dug wells so that the people could have clean water.

'I can manage, Dad,' Tilly told her dad, 'you don't need to send us away. I can keep things tidy and I've learnt to cook quite a few things at school. Toby and Alfie will help, won't you?' she asked them, and they nodded. 'Please let us stay here; don't send us away to Aunt Eliza,' she begged.

The children's father sighed. 'I'm sorry, kids. I would worry all day, and so will Mum when she wakes up—six weeks is too long for you to manage here on your own. I don't even think the authorities would allow it, anyway. They would probably decide you had to go into foster care, and who knows who you would be put with. I'd much rather you stayed together and went to my aunt. I know she seems to be a bit strict, but she has a heart of gold underneath her severe expression. You'll just have to work a bit to find it. I used to stay with her when I was your age. I had heaps of fun playing in the river and her huge garden. I'm going to phone her and see what she says. If she agrees, I'll take you down as soon as school breaks up.'

'How can we work hard to find her heart of gold?' Alfie asked. 'I don't know what you mean.'

Their dad sat down on the settee, pulling Alfie onto his lap, and putting his arm around Toby and Tilly as they sat each side of him.

'Love is the way into everyone's heart, Alfie,' he explained. 'Life can be hard for all of us—just like now, with Mum so ill and us not knowing if she will get better and, if she does, whether she will be able to speak properly or use her arms and legs. When things are hard, sometimes we get angry, and being angry makes a shell around our hearts. We stop letting people come near us, and only love can melt that shell. When love does that, the real person can shine out again. Aunt Eliza had a very sad and difficult life, and that made her build a shell around her heart. She won't tell you about the bad times, so don't ask her—but try to be patient and loving and helpful. Maybe you will begin to discover the gold in her heart.

'Now that is a holiday project for you! Look after each other well and enjoy the wonderful place where she lives. I'll phone you every night when I get back from the hospital and talk to you and tell you about Mum. I'll put money on your phone, Tilly, and we'll use that to keep in touch. I'll expect lots of texts, too, to cheer Mummy and me up. We all have to be brave and that will help her recovery. And I want you all to pray every night for each of us, including Aunt Eliza, that we will be strong and come through this difficult time.'

The children were quiet for a few moments, then Tilly promised her dad she would pray, and the boys agreed.

'It's going to be like an adventure, and sometimes adventures are scary,' said Toby, 'but we'll stick together and be a team and be as good as we can.'

'That's my boy!' said his dad, smiling and hugging all the children again. 'Now off to bed with you all, while I phone my aunt. It will be a shock and a challenge for her, too—don't forget that,' he added.

That evening, all the arrangements were made for the children to be taken down the following Saturday to stay in the village of Nottington, near Weymouth, in rural Dorset. It would be quite a change from the outskirts of the city of Bristol!

Chapter three

Eliza sat down in her wicker rocking chair, her legs shaking. How was she going to manage? She was now 77 years old and would have three noisy young children in her house for six whole weeks! Of course, she could have told her nephew, David, 'No way!', but she didn't have the heart to do that. When he had phoned a few days before to tell her about his wife, she had been terribly upset; she was very fond of David and Alice.

After all, she reminded herself, she did have a large house and garden—plenty of room for the children to sleep and play. Her 'help', as she called Ann, the young woman from the village who cleaned the house each week, might be willing to work some extra hours, and perhaps her children would play with her great-nephews and great-niece sometimes. Maybe it would work out.

Eliza sat rocking for a while. She was scared—she had to admit that to herself. Fancy an old woman being scared of three children! If only she was more like her sister, who had always loved the children being around her and had so wanted to have more than just the one son she had been blessed with.

What did twenty-first-century children do to amuse themselves? she asked herself. She had no Internet connection because she didn't own a computer, but she had heard that children had things called 'tablets' on which they played games. There was a TV in the lounge, but it was quite small and old. Would the children be bored living in a village which had no shops, no bus service and very few other children? David had always been happy when he stayed with her, but he was of a different generation.

Then there was the question of food. How would she feed them all and what would they like? Eliza walked up to the main Dorchester Road and caught a bus to town every few weeks, bought her food and the supermarket delivered it to her home. She decided that she would have to go the next day and do a big shop. Maybe she had better phone her 'help', Ann, and get her advice.

That proved to be a good idea.

'I should buy sausages and fish fingers, and mince to make chilli and cottage pies. Children usually love spaghetti—my children like pasta in all shapes and sizes. You can buy lots of ready-made sauces to put with mince, and you need tins of tomatoes to go with it, and grated cheese for the top,' Ann helpfully told her.

'I can certainly help you get ready for their visit,' she added. 'Would you like me to come over in the morning? I could drive you to the supermarket, help you do a shop and then, when I bring you home, I can make up the beds and we could work on a menu plan. It's a free day for me, so as soon as I've taken the children to school I can come round and help until it's time to pick them up.'

Tears welled up in Eliza's eyes. 'Would you really be able to do that?' she said. 'It would be such a weight off my shoulders. I'm happy to pay for your petrol as well as your time.'

'Don't even think about it!' replied Ann. 'It's a terrible situation for your nephew and his family, and I'm only too pleased to be able to help. I'll do what I can to help you through the holidays and I'm sure my kids will enjoy having new friends to play with, too. There aren't many children in the village these days.'

The days that followed passed quickly for both Aunt Eliza and the family as they prepared for the next few weeks. Ann was brilliant, and she helped Eliza cook some recipes she thought the children would love, so the freezer was soon stocked, as well as the cake and biscuit tins. Ann's son and daughter, Charlie and Poppy, who were 10 and 8 years old, sought out some puzzles, games and books to loan the family while they were there and were excited about meeting Tilly, Toby and Alfie.

Saturday arrived, and after breakfast the children piled in the car, glad that it was quite large and there was plenty of room for their cases and even their bikes. Dad had bought a bike rack and fixed it on the back, as well as a roof rack for a tent and sleeping bags, thinking it would be fun for the children to camp in the field, just as he had done when he had stayed with his aunt so many years before. He prayed that his aunt would cope well and that the children would grow to love her, just as he had done.

The journey took just over two hours. The family had made an early start because the roads were often busy on the first day of the school holidays, especially in the West Country, where many people liked to go for holidays. The morning was sunny and warm and, in spite of the difficult situation, Tilly found her spirits lifting. Maybe it would work out all right.

They drove around the town of Dorchester, then along the main road leading to Weymouth. Their dad then took a turning into Upwey, a village which had been absorbed into the suburbs of Weymouth. It was the source of the river Wey. As they travelled their dad told them about the places through which they passed—Upwey and Broadwey—and then they turned off into a very small road which led them to Nottington.

The first building they saw was very strange. It was octagonal and very pretty. Next to it was a row of what looked like cottages, with a larger house at the end. This house had grand stone pelicans on the gateposts, and it was here that Dad stopped the car.

'We're here!' their dad informed them as he turned off the engine. 'Tilly, will you go through the little gate, please, and ring the doorbell, to let Aunt Eliza know we're here? Then she'll open the main gate and I'll drive in so that we can unload.'

Tilly felt rather apprehensive as she unlatched the gate, went up to the door and pressed the old-fashioned bell. The door opened almost immediately. Aunt Eliza was standing there and smiling. It wasn't the sort of smile her nan gave her, but at least it was a smile.

'We'd better open the double gates, then, and let your father in,' Aunt Eliza said, in her rather clipped voice.

Dad drove in. Tilly could see that behind the garage was an amazing garden. She wanted to run off and explore straight away, but she knew she should help unpack the car and be polite.

'Please let me take that,' she said to Aunt Eliza, who had taken one of the cases. 'We'll bring everything in.'

'Oh, thank you, Tilly,' her great-aunt replied. 'I'll go and put the kettle on, then. I'm sure your father would like a cup of coffee after the journey, and maybe you children would like some lemonade?'

'That sounds wonderful, Auntie,' Tilly said, 'and thank you for having us to stay while Mummy is in hospital.'

'I think we'll all get on very well together,' Eliza said, trying to smile at the family, though feeling very scared and shaky inside.

And so began a summer holiday which none of them would ever forget.

Chapter four

*D*avid stayed around for a little while helping his children settle into his aunt's home. It was such an unusual house, having once been part of a much larger building. There were three storeys and the children were to sleep on the top floor. When they saw their bedrooms, they were delighted. From the window of the back room they were able to look out over the river Wey and across the meadows to the farmhouse in the distance. Tilly chose this room, while the boys shared the other room, which looked out over the lovely octagonal building and down into the village.

'I'll tell you all about the house one day,' promised Aunt Eliza. The children had been asking so many questions that her head was buzzing. 'Why don't you go and explore the garden while I talk to your father,' she suggested. 'Please don't go through the gate which has steps down to the river, though—I don't want anyone getting wet today! We'll talk about river rules later.'

'Rules?' Toby muttered as they went out of the back door. 'I hate rules and regulations. Do you think Aunt Eliza will have lots of rules we have to obey?'

'Don't start getting cross,' said Tilly, 'I expect it's just to keep us safe with the river so near. Look! It's flowing right beside the house.'

The river wasn't very wide but it flowed quite fast and it was difficult to see how deep it might be. It wound its way along the edge of the meadow where the cows were grazing, carried on round a bend and flowed alongside the houses, and then seemed to disappear.

The garden was large—or so it seemed to the children who were used to a small back garden at home. They walked to the far side and over a little wooden bridge into a paddock.

'This must be where Daddy thought we could pitch the tent and have an outside sleepover,' said Alfie in excitement. 'I do hope Auntie lets us do that—she won't have a rule about not sleeping in the tent, will she?'

'Daddy said he used to camp outside when he was a boy, so I'm sure it'll be fine,' Tilly said, hoping her words were true. 'There are some good trees to climb if we're allowed,' she added.

The little bridge they had crossed went over a ditch which was almost dry. Toby thought that in winter when it was wet it would be a stream, an overflow from the river.

'I think this is a fun place to stay,' stated Alfie. 'If only Mummy and Daddy were here with us.'

'It *will* be fun,' Toby said firmly. 'We'll make it fun, and we'll be a team and try to melt Auntie's heart with love, like Daddy said. We could make a den outside somewhere and every day pray for Mummy to get better.'

'What a good idea,' said Tilly. 'It could be our secret place. We'd better ask Aunt Eliza if she minds us building one, though. We don't want to upset her as soon as we've arrived.'

'Time for lunch!' called their dad from the back door, and they raced back to the house.

'It's an amazing garden!' announced Toby. 'We want to build a den in the top part of the garden.'

'Steady on,' replied their father, 'this is Aunt Eliza's garden and she may not want that.'

'I'll think about it,' she called from the kitchen. 'We'll talk later about what you may or may not do. First, go and wash your hands and come to the dining room—it's the room behind the kitchen.'

The dining room seemed rather grand to the children. On the walls were large paintings of important-looking people who seemed to peer down at them, watching every mouthful they ate. Their dad began to explain who they were—some of their ancestors. It made Tilly think she must be careful about her manners and watch her brothers. She remembered how once, when Aunt Eliza was visiting them, she had recited a little poem to Toby, who had been much younger then:

'Toby Porter, strong and able,

Take your elbows off the table!'

Tilly couldn't help giggling a little, and her great-aunt frowned at her.

'If you find something funny, then tell us all,' she said.

'It's nothing, Auntie,' Tilly hastily replied. 'I was just thinking about those ancestors watching us.'

After lunch, their dad had to leave and go to the hospital. They waved him goodbye from the front porch, all feeling sad and mixed-up inside. It had been OK while their dad was with them, but now they were alone in this strange house with an old great-aunt they hardly knew.

'I need to rest for a little while,' she told them. 'Why don't you unpack your things, then find something to do.

There are some games and books which have been loaned to you for the holidays. Mind you take care of them, as they belong to Poppy and Charlie. They are the children of the lady who helps me in the house, and they want to come and make friends with you while you're here.'

'Thank you, Auntie,' said Tilly. 'We'll do the washing up for you, if you like, and we'll be quiet, so you can rest.'

'Thank you, Tilly,' answered Aunt Eliza, 'that is a kind offer.' She smiled at the children and they went back inside the house to clear the dishes. The kitchen was very different from their one at home, but still cosy and homely. The big Aga cooker was a mystery to Tilly and she didn't know how to use it, even to boil a kettle. As she looked around, she was glad to see an electric kettle on the worktop. She spotted a dishwasher, too, and decided to put the dishes into that, hoping Aunt Eliza wouldn't mind. Once it was loaded, she hunted for some tablets for it, and found a utility room where they were stored.

Leading from the kitchen was a 'snug'—a small sitting room with an open fireplace, a comfy settee and armchairs. A small TV was on a cupboard. It looked cosy and inviting.

Eliza went to her bedroom and lay down, letting out a huge sigh. What had she let herself in for? David's children were pleasant and helpful, but already she was tired, and they had only been with her for one morning! Talking to David she had discovered how very serious his wife's illness was and the possibility that she might not recover, or might recover only partially, remaining an invalid for the rest of her life. David had explained that only by a miracle could she recover fully, and he and the family were praying for that to happen.

Prayer—Eliza thought about how long it was since she had prayed or even thought about God. Could He do a miracle for Alice? Would He help her to cope?

When she was young she had gone to Sunday school and learnt about Jesus and how to pray, but that was so many years ago. She sat up on her bed and closed her eyes, thinking quietly:

'God, if you are there, would you help us all? I'm sorry that I have neglected you for most of my life, and I don't know how to pray. I can't get down on my knees any more—or if I did, I'd probably need to call 999 for someone to help me get up! Does it matter if I talk to you sitting up on my bed? Please help me to cope—I know that's selfish, but I don't much like children and I feel too old to learn how to understand them. Most of all I pray—for David and the children's sake—please heal Alice completely. Amen.'

Having prayed, Eliza lay down again and fell asleep at once for a whole hour. She awoke feeling refreshed and much less worried.

'God must have heard me!' she thought.

Chapter five

After a few days, Tilly, Toby and Alfie began to feel quite at home in Nottington. They had quickly made friends with Poppy and Charlie, been out for cycle rides with them and played in the garden. Aunt Eliza's rules were not so terrible after all—actually, they were rather sensible, Tilly thought, although the boys didn't altogether agree:

1. Breakfast at 8 a.m., lunch at 1 p.m. and dinner at 6.30 p.m.—please don't be late! (No problem for the boys—they were always hungry!)
2. No one is to wander off on their own—and never to go into the river or off on a cycle ride without telling me.
3. Everyone must make their own bed and keep their bedroom tidy (I'm too old to climb to the top floor very often!).
4. There is a rota in the kitchen for helping set the table, clearing the dishes, washing up and feeding the ducks.

In the middle of the week, the weather suddenly changed and there were several thunderstorms. Alfie hated thunder, Tilly didn't like the lightning but Toby wanted to be outdoors even though it was pouring with rain. Aunt Eliza didn't know how to entertain them. They played some board games for a while but started to argue about who was winning. Then a thought struck her. She knew the attic needed tidying up but she hadn't managed to get up there for years. Maybe the children would like to do that—they had been very helpful with other jobs around the house and garden.

'I've had an idea,' she said. 'It's too wet to go outside but there is something I've wanted to do for years but I've not been able to get there. From Toby and Alfie's room you can get into the attic, and it needs a good tidy-up. I'm just too old and too fat to get through the trap door and sort things out. You'll need to put on old clothes because it'll be dirty and dusty. And I hope none of you are scared of spiders, because I'm sure some will live up in the roof.

'Actually, my attic spreads across the house next door as well. It was never changed when the big house was made into smaller ones, and as next door are away on holiday, it won't matter if you're noisy.

'There's an electric light—the switch is near the opening, but you may need torches as well. You can explore all you like, but if you could make a list for me of what is up there and make sure it's tidy, that would be a great help. In fact,' she added, 'it will definitely be a pocket money job—I would have to pay a handyman to get up there.'

Toby jumped up at once. 'Can we start now?' he asked. 'I'd love to do that.'

The others agreed, put the game away and ran upstairs. Aunt Eliza went up behind them. Her knees didn't like the three flights of stairs and the exercise made her puff. However, she needed to show the children how to get into the attic and make sure they had torches and a broom.

They went into the room where the boys slept, and Tilly, Toby and Alfie all looked up at the ceiling to see where the opening to the attic was. Unlike in their house, however, they couldn't see any trap door.

Aunt Eliza laughed—a deep-down chuckle which surprised the children, as they hadn't heard their great-aunt laugh before.

'This is why I had to climb all those stairs,' she said, 'because now we have to move that huge chest of drawers to find the secret door. It's heavy, but the four of us can manage it.'

'Secret door?' said Toby. 'Wow! That sounds really exciting!'

Together they managed to move the furniture, revealing a small door with a little latch handle.

'It's like in the Narnia stories!' Tilly exclaimed. 'The children went through the back of a wardrobe, but we'll have our own adventures behind a chest of drawers!'

'I hadn't thought of it like that,' said Aunt Eliza, 'but goodness knows what you'll discover up there.'

Toby had opened the tiny door to find a wooden staircase behind which led straight up to a trap door in the attic floor.

'Can I go first?' Toby asked, and his great-aunt agreed.

'When you get to the top of the stairs, push the trap door upwards—it has a hinge. Once it's fully opened you'll find the light switch on the left-hand side.'

'Got it,' Toby shouted back, and the light came on.

'Now,' Aunt Eliza instructed, 'there's a hook to secure the trap door—fix that first, so that it stays open while you're up there. I'm going downstairs again, so if you need anything, one of you will have to come and find me. Have fun, and tidy it up for me!'

Despite the electric light, it was still quite dark in the attic. When all three children were inside, they used their torches to see how large the space was and decide where they needed to start with the tidying.

'I think this must have been a room, once upon a time,' Tilly remarked. 'The whole space has a proper floor and the floorboards have been stained. And look over there at that wall—it looks as if there was once a window which has since been bricked up.'

'Let's start sorting next door's side,' suggested Alfie. 'If we get lots of wet days and want to be up here, at least we'll have done that end before the neighbours come back from their holiday.'

'That's a good idea,' Tilly responded. 'We need to have a plan. When we open any boxes we'll make a list of what is in them, so that Auntie can decide what she wants to keep or throw away.'

The first couple of boxes weren't very interesting. They contained old plates and kitchen utensils, but the children carefully recorded what they discovered, even though a few items were so old that even Tilly didn't know what they were called or used for, so she tried to draw them. Then they found a box with old toys. There was a clockwork train set which the boys wanted to put together to see if it worked. While they did that, Tilly tried to pull out a tea chest. It wasn't very heavy, but it was a bit awkward, and in the effort of trying to free it she lost her balance and fell back against the wall. Her foot got caught by a loose brick, and as she tried to release it, hoping she hadn't sprained her ankle, she realized that there was something behind the brick: a cavity. Tilly quickly put on her torch and looked inside. At the back of the cavity she saw an old book. She pulled it out carefully. It was very dusty, and when she opened it she realized that it was some sort of a diary.

'Hey boys,' she called. Toby and Alfie stopped playing with the train set and came over. 'Look what I've found! It was hidden behind a loose brick in the wall. My foot got caught and moved the brick. There was a cavity behind it and this was hidden there. I think it's someone's diary. Isn't it exciting!'

'I'd rather have the train set—that's more fun than a dusty old book,' commented Alfie. 'But a secret hiding place is exciting. Are you sure there's nothing else hidden there—like jewels or gold coins?'

'I flashed the torch around and I don't think there's anything else—but you can look again if you like.'

The cavity was empty, much to the boys' disappointment, so they went back to playing with the train set.

'I wonder if Daddy played with this train set when he came to stay with Aunt Eliza?' Toby said. 'I'll ask him when he phones tonight.'

'Anyway, it's almost lunch time,' remarked Tilly, looking at her watch. 'We'd better go downstairs and wash our hands. Let's leave the trap door open and come back here this afternoon. I'm going to take the diary downstairs and show it to Aunt Eliza.'

Over lunch they talked about what they had found in the attic and they showed Aunt Eliza the diary.

'Tilly, since you found it, I think you should be the custodian of the diary,' she said. 'Read it and tell us what it's all about.'

After lunch, the weather began to clear a little and Charlie and Poppy arrived on their bikes.

'We baked some cupcakes this morning,' Poppy told them, 'and we brought some round for your tea. Can you come out for a bike ride?

'Well,' answered Toby, 'we were going back up to the attic; we've been tidying it up for Auntie. It's a sort of secret place, but you could help us.'

'I suggest you all go for a bike ride now,' said Aunt Eliza, 'then you can come back later and go up to the attic. It's good to get some fresh air. Where were you thinking of going?' she asked Charlie.

'To Upwey,' he answered. 'I thought we should show Tilly, Toby and Alfie where the river begins.'

'That sounds like a very good idea,' Aunt Eliza said. 'If you come back around 4 p.m. you can have those lovely-looking cakes and a drink and still have time to go up to the attic for a couple of hours before dinner.'

It was a good idea and the five children enjoyed the ride to Upwey. They went into the Wishing Well gardens to see the beginning of the river Wey. A wishing well had been built at the source of the river many years earlier, and they marvelled at how many people had thrown in coins and made a wish.

'Does it really work?' Alfie asked. 'I'd throw in every bit of my pocket money if I thought a wish would make Mummy wake up and get better.'

'I don't think wishes like that really work; it's a sort of tradition, a bit like making a wish as you blow out birthday candles,' answered Tilly. 'But praying is different, because you're asking God, and He can do everything. That's why Daddy asked us to pray every day.'

There were some benches near the wishing well and the children squeezed onto one of them.

'Tell us about the attic,' said Charlie. 'It sounds like you had fun.'

'We did,' replied Toby. 'You have to go through this secret door in our bedroom, up some tiny stairs and through a trap door, and there's this huge attic. It covers Aunt Eliza's house and the one next door. We started to tidy and list what was in the boxes at the neighbours' end, 'cos they've gone on holiday and Auntie said it wouldn't matter if we made a noise.'

'It was so cool being up there,' Alfie told them. 'Kind of a bit spooky at first, and not much light, but in one box we found a wind-up railway and we got it going. Then Tilly got her foot caught and kicked open a secret hiding place in the wall!'

'Yes, inside the hole there was an old diary, which I'm going to read and then tell everyone what I find out,' added Tilly.

'You're so lucky staying in an old house with secrets,' Charlie said enviously. 'Our house is only ten years old and has nowhere to explore and have adventures.'

'But you and Poppy can share ours,' Toby said at once. 'You're our friends, and friends share. You can stay and explore with us. I'd like to explore more of Upwey—it looks a nice village.'

31

They left the wishing well and followed the river through the village, stopping from time to time to look at the old buildings and the bridges which used to carry the old railway over the roads.

'Watch out!' shouted Charlie, as they cycled round a sharp bend and almost straight into the river at Broadwey. 'Sorry, I forgot to warn you about that!'

They had to leave the riverside and cycle down the main road for a while, before they turned off into Nottington Lane and back to Aunt Eliza's house.

Aunt Eliza had enjoyed her time of peace and quiet, waking up refreshed, and was quite surprised to find she was looking forward to all the children coming back for tea. Her life was far less lonely now with three and sometimes five children in her home.

Chapter six

That evening, Aunt Eliza decided to tell the children
a little about the history of her house. It was called
'Greystones' because it was built with Portland stone that
had a grey colour.

'The pelicans on the gateposts came from the old
manor house, which once belonged to our family but was
demolished many, many years ago. The large oil paintings
of our ancestors were also in the old house—they suited
the grand old house. Greystones is an interesting house,
with all sorts of nooks and crannies, but it's only part of
what was once a large house belonging to the octagonal
Spa House. The spa spring was thought to have healing
properties, and back in the past people came to bathe in
the water. King George III came to bathe here when he
stayed at Weymouth each summer, to improve his health.

'The Spa House itself was built around 1830, so that
people had a better place in which to bathe. It had a
pump room, where people could drink the spring water;
two bathrooms; a dressing room; two sitting rooms and
six bedrooms. Now it has been turned into a lovely family
house.

'Then this large house was built next to the Spa House
as a boarding house where people could come and stay
while they had treatment at the spa. It had ten bedrooms,
a nursery, five reception rooms, a kitchen, a scullery, a
laundry and a pantry so that they could look after all the

guests, plus a coach house and a stable for three horses. Greystones used to be part of the coach house and stables, and where the big window in the lounge now is, there used to be an archway where the carriages would come into the courtyard and stable. It's hard to imagine that, isn't it?'

'It is, Aunt Eliza,' said Alfie. 'But what's a scullery and a pantry?'

'Sorry, I should have explained better! In the olden days the kitchen was just for cooking. All the preparation of the vegetables, which would have been grown in the walled garden where you play now, would have been done in the scullery. The pantry was a cool room where food was stored as it was long before fridges and freezers were invented. Oh, and "reception rooms" were the rooms where you received guests—so they included sitting rooms and dining rooms.

'When bathing in the spa and "taking the waters", as they called drinking the spring water, went out of fashion the large boarding house was divided up into several cottages and our large house with the garden here at the end.

'One Sunday we'll go up to Radipole Church, because we're in that parish and there are memorials to your ancestors on the walls,' Aunt Eliza added.

'At home we go to Breakfast Church on Sundays, and we have sausages and bacon butties and sing and hear stories,' said Toby. 'Do you have breakfast at your church?'

'I've never heard of such a thing—no, definitely not. I believe you can get drinks and biscuits afterwards in the old school opposite the church. Will that do?' Aunt Eliza asked them.

'Of course it will,' Tilly reassured her. 'It will be a new experience, and Daddy always says it's cool for us to experience new things. In fact, he told us that when we started to go to Breakfast Church last year. We didn't want to go as we'd never been to church before, but we love it now, and we can still go out and do lots of other things afterwards.'

'It's a long time since I went to church, but we'll plan on going on Sunday,' decided Aunt Eliza.

Tilly's mobile began to ring, so she ran to get it from the table. 'It'll be Daddy,' she said, as she answered it. She turned the speaker on so that everyone could hear the news and chat.

'How are you all?' asked their dad. 'What have you been doing today?'

Everyone tried to speak at once until their father told them to speak to him in age order, the youngest first and ending with Aunt Eliza.

There was a lot to tell him that day, especially about the diary found in the secret hiding place. When everyone had talked to him, Dad then announced, 'Well, I've got some good news at last! The doctors think it's time to wake Mummy up from her coma and see if her brain is recovering. She may be paralysed down one side and not be able to talk, but until she's woken up, no one will know. She'll wake up slowly, over a few days, so that means I won't come down to see you until after she's awake and we know how she's getting on. Is that OK with you all?' he asked.

Tilly took the phone. 'We do understand,' she told their dad, 'but don't worry about us. Aunt Eliza is wonderful to us and we've made friends with Charlie and Poppy and are having lots of fun. I can't wait to read the diary and tell you about it. When Mummy wakes up, tell her we love her—and we miss you both,' she added.

Tilly glanced at her great-aunt, who had tears in her eyes.

'What's the matter, Auntie?' she said, running over to her and putting her arm around her. 'Are we too much for you to look after?'

'Oh no, dear, it's nothing like that. It's just that—well, no one's ever called me "wonderful" before. I felt a little overcome. Sorry, I'm just a silly old lady, aren't I?'

'But you are wonderful,' said Toby, 'and we all love you! You're really cool for an old lady!'

'I'll take that as a compliment, young man!' she said, still a bit teary. 'Like Alfie, I'm learning the meaning of some new words today!'

They all began to laugh, and Aunt Eliza felt better than she had for years—almost young once more.

That night, Tilly couldn't wait to get to bed! Her brothers joined her in her room each bedtime to pray for their mum—they had been learning in church about God, who was their heavenly Father, and how they could talk to Him anytime about anything, and that was what prayer was all about. So they just told God how they felt and asked Him to make their mum better and to look after Dad, and they also said 'thank you' for Aunt Eliza looking after them, their new friends and the fun they had had that day.

'I'm glad we go to "Sausage Church" on Sundays,' Alfie said when they finished talking to God. 'I hope Aunt Eliza's church will be good, too.'

'I think it will be different, but we can still talk to God and sing to Him,' Toby answered.

'We'll enjoy it for Auntie's sake—remember, we have to love her to bits like Daddy told us,' Tilly reminded them, as the boys left for their bedroom.

She snuggled down in her bed and reached for the diary. The writing was a little faint, but with the help of her torch, the curtains open and the light on, she managed to read:

This is my new book. Papa suggests that I use it as a diary.

Today is March 10th, in the year of our Lord 1850.

My name is Mabel Louisa Henderson and I am 11 years old. I live in the Spa Boarding House in Nottington, Dorset, England, with my Mama, Papa and now a tiny baby brother, Hamish Sebastian. He is one month old, but was born too early, so is very small.

I haven't seen Hamish yet, because I am confined to the nursery on the second floor as I have scarlet fever and it has made my heart and my kidneys very weak. I cough a lot and have become very thin, and the doctor fears that I may have developed consumption, too. If I were to infect Hamish, he might not be strong enough to fight the infection.

I hate being shut up in the nursery. The scullery maid, Violet, has been given the new job of being my helper and companion. She calls me 'Mab', which I like much better

than 'Mabel'; and I call her 'Vi', because her family call her
that. Vi's family live in the village, but while she takes care
of me Papa thought it would be best if she lived upstairs
in our attic room. He didn't want her to be far away if I
needed anything, and she has lots of small brothers and
sisters and we don't want them to get sick.

I look out of my bedroom window and the river is just
below me. How I wish I could go down the steps and into
the water for a swim or row the boat upstream to the farm!
I miss the river! I can just see the mallard ducks. They are
almost like my pets, they are so tame. I must remember to
ask Vi to feed them. The farmer gives me grain from time
to time and the ducks love it. They come right up to the
back door at meal times. The groom (who is Vi's brother
and looks after the horses) is very mean and shoos them
away.

I have been confined to my bedroom for six weeks now.
It seems for ever! Papa comes up to see me every evening
and brings me little presents. Cook sometimes comes with
little treats she has baked to encourage me to eat more.
Yesterday she brought some maids of honour cakes, and
even though they are my favourites I only managed to eat
half of one cake. I hate to disappoint her, but I am just not
hungry. I think I need to get out and run around and get
some fresh air, but no one agrees with me or will let me. I
get Vi to open the window, but all the grown-ups who come
to visit tut-tut and shut it very quickly!

I miss school, too. I miss my friends who are not allowed
to visit me, and I miss the lessons, especially history and
geography. Vi has never been to school, so I am trying to
teach her how to read. It helps pass the time and she learns

very quickly. She tells me that Queen Victoria wants all children to go to school and learn to read and write. None of her family have ever been to school except to Sunday school classes.

Now, dear Diary, I am tired so will stop writing and have my rest. Goodnight!

Tilly was feeling tired too, so she closed the diary and put out the light. She thought about Mab having to stay upstairs day and night for weeks, probably sleeping in the same room that was her bedroom for the holiday, looking at the same river Wey from the same window. It seemed weird somehow, but she felt she was entering someone else's life and story; as if she was the one meant to find the diary and read it; as if it had been written just for her. Tilly wondered if Toby and Alfie would understand that— they would probably just think she was being silly. She gave a sigh, turned over and fell asleep.

Chapter seven

The weekend was approaching, and the weather had improved a lot. Although they had enjoyed the adventure in the attic, they all decided that they would rather be outside while it was sunny and warm. Aunt Eliza needed to go shopping. She was now beginning to enjoy looking after her young guests but found they did have very healthy appetites. Her 'help', Ann, had been as good as her word and found extra time to come to Greystones to work. They had made another meal plan for the coming week, along with suggestions from the children, and decided to go to Weymouth. There was no room for all five children in her car, so they had been allowed to cycle. They all had helmets and were sensible. The main road had a cycle lane, so Aunt Eliza was sure they would be safe. They planned to play on the beach and meet at the Nothe Fort Gardens for a picnic lunch.

Once the shopping was finished, the two ladies drove up to the Nothe Gardens and sat enjoying a coffee, looking out over the harbour.

'How are you managing?' Ann asked Eliza. 'Are the children behaving well? They seem nice kids and my two love being with them.'

'You know,' answered Eliza, 'I was so scared when my nephew asked me to look after them. I've had so little to do with children, and things are so different now from when I grew up, but once we got used to each other it was fine. It's nice to have some noise and life in the old house, although I do get tired quickly. They are helpful, though, and very respectful—I think David and Alice have done a great job bringing them up. I wish I wasn't so worried about Alice—what will happen if she is paralysed and unable to speak after this massive stroke? How will they all manage?'

'It's terrible to think about,' replied Ann, 'but you just have to take one day at a time. There have been so many advances in modern medicine. We've been praying for you all and have put Alice's name on our church prayer list. I've learnt in recent years that God does hear us and answer our prayers, even though not always in the way we expect.'

'I lost my faith in God years ago,' said Eliza a little sadly, 'but the children have made me think about Him again, for they pray for their mother every night. At home they go to a "Sausage Church", as Alfie calls it—I gather it's informal and they eat breakfast there, but they seem to love it, from what they say. I've promised to take them with me to St Ann's in Radipole on Sunday. It'll be very different from what they've experienced before, but I can show them the plaques on the wall about their ancestors, and maybe even the family graves.'

'I'm sure they'll find it interesting,' said Ann. 'Let me know how you get on. Meanwhile, isn't it lovely to enjoy some peace and quiet and this wonderful view!'

Charlie had taken charge of the cycle ride as he knew the route well. At a certain point they left the main Dorchester Road and cycled along the side of Radipole Lake, where the river Wey enters a marshy area with lots of reeds. It had been made into a nature reserve. When they reached

41

a large car park, the children stopped, locked their bikes and explored the nature reserve.

'How do you know the names of all the ducks and birds?' Toby asked his friend. 'I don't know any apart from the swans. Look at that one: it must be the mum, there are five cygnets behind her—aren't they cute! This is such a cool place to visit! Thanks for bringing us here.'

'We once went on a school trip to a place called Slimbridge, an amazing bird sanctuary,' replied Charlie. 'I loved it and afterwards got a book from the library to learn more about wildfowl. Now I come down here quite often and also go to the Lodmoor nature reserve. I'll take you there another day—it's not far from here. I want to work with wildlife when I grow up,' he added.

'I've already finished year 7 and I have no idea what I want to do for a career,' said Tilly. 'Lots of my friends know and are working out the choices they'll make for GCSEs. It worries me a bit, but I can't think of anything I'd really like to do for years and years.'

'Don't worry, Sis,' said Alfie, giving his sister a smile. 'Daddy says we mustn't worry, 'cos God has it all planned out and we just have to ask Him.'

'Wow!' exclaimed Poppy, looking at her watch, 'look at the time! We'd better cycle over to the Nothe Gardens and meet Mum and your auntie. Don't know about you, but I'm starving already.'

A few minutes later the children were back on their bikes and cycling along the old boat-train track around Weymouth harbour. When they reached the Town Bridge, they had to dismount and wait as it was being raised to allow boats to go through to the outer harbour. It was fun to watch so they didn't mind the delay. Tilly took photos on her phone to send to her dad and mum, so they could see where they had been. Once all the boats had passed out of the marina, other boats came from the other side to enter the inner harbour and moor up.

After the bridge had closed again they pushed their bikes over it and went down through narrow lanes and past some very old buildings, then up a steep hill to reach the Nothe Gardens. Charlie sent a text to his mum to ask where she was waiting, and they soon found her.

After walking up the hill they were all ready for a cold drink and their picnic lunch, before exploring the gardens and the outside of Nothe Fort.

'I wonder why everything tastes so much better when you eat it outside,' commented Tilly, munching some crisps. 'I love picnics.'

Aunt Eliza laughed. 'You're just like I was as a girl. I was always nagging my mother to make picnics, even if we just ate them in the garden. It's years since I last ate outside. I think we must do it more often. I was thinking about that den you want to make in the garden. If you make it in the top field, you could have the tent there as well and have picnics. If it's fine when your father comes, you could even make a camp fire and cook sausages.'

'Yay!' shouted Alfie. 'You have the best ideas, Auntie. I love staying with you!'

Aunt Eliza beamed to hear that; she thought it was one of the nicest things anyone had said to her for years. She noticed, though, that Charlie and Poppy were looking a little sad.

'Cheer up, you two,' she said. 'You can come and camp too, if your parents will allow it.'

'Please say we can,' Poppy begged her mum.

'We'll check it's OK with Dad, but I'm sure he won't mind at all,' answered Ann. 'Maybe you can take Spot, he's such a good guard dog. Now, here's some money—you can all go round the Nothe Fort. There's so much to explore there. You'll be able to leave your bikes locked at the entrance—I've checked that's OK. Just remember to keep together—we don't want anyone getting lost in the tunnels! You need to leave here by half past four at the latest, so that you're home in good time for your meal. You're all coming to our house for supper this evening—it'll give your Aunt Eliza a day off from cooking.'

The two women went back to the car and the children took their bikes to the fort entrance. The fort had been built as a sea defence in the Napoleonic Wars. The army had used it up until the end of the Second World War, and now it was a museum-cum-theme park. Charlie and Poppy had visited it lots of times and never got tired of playing there. Poppy was glad to have Tilly with her: the boys raced to look at the tank and the guns, while the girls started on a mouse hunt—trying to spot mice which had been hidden in different places.

The time went very quickly. They all enjoyed the visit very much and ended it by buying ice creams with the pocket money Aunt Eliza had given her great-niece and great-nephews. Then they just had enough time to walk through the gardens to a little cove, called Newton's Cove, and paddle in the rock pools. Once again, Charlie was able to tell them about the crabs, limpets and other little creatures they saw there.

'We'll come with our shrimping nets next time,' he told them enthusiastically.

They cycled home rather slowly, all of them a little tired after all the fun of the day. However, there was more fun to come, for when they reached Charlie and Poppy's home, there was a wonderful smell coming from the garden.

'We're having a barbeque!' said Charlie. 'Dad must be home and cooking it.'

'Sausages!' said Alfie, sniffing appreciatively. 'I love sausages!'

It was such fun, and afterwards, while everyone was still sitting in the garden, Aunt Eliza asked Tilly to tell them what she had read in the diary. She told them about Mab and Vi.

'I think I might be too tired to read any more this evening,' she told them, with a big yawn. 'It's been such a fun day!'

At this point her mobile rang. It was her dad, wanting to tell them the news:

'Mummy opened her eyes today, and she smiled at me! The doctor says that is very good news—it means she recognized me, so that part of her brain is working!'

Everyone shouted at once into the phone, they were all so happy. When their dad had rung off, after hearing all about their day, they were all quiet and Ann and her husband suggested that they all say 'thank you' to God together and pray for continued healing. It was a lovely way to finish a very special day.

Chapter eight

O nce in bed, Tilly thought she would get to sleep very
quickly because it had been such a busy and exciting
day, but she found her mind was going round and round
thinking about her mum. After a while she got up, put
on the light and took the diary off the bedside table and
began to read.

'Dear Diary,' Mab had written on a new page,

*I haven't felt very well for a few days, so didn't feel like
writing to you. Last night, after he had visited me, I
overheard Papa telling Vi that when I left the nursery
floor all my belongings would have to be burnt, because
of the danger of infection. This made me so unhappy that
I couldn't sleep. Some things don't matter very much, but
other things are special treasures which I don't want to be
put into a fire to be burnt. I'm sure that after a while any
germs will die, and they will be quite safe to use again.*

*When Vi arrived this morning to help me wash and be
ready for breakfast, she could see that I was upset.*

'Whatever's the matter, Mab?' she asked.

Tears began to come to my eyes again.

*'I overheard Papa talking to you last night,' I told her,
'and I want to keep some of my things safe. You understand
that it must be our secret. We will gather my special
treasures together and you must hide them somewhere. If
I don't get better (and there are some days when I feel that*

could happen), then you will have to look after them for me.
Can you agree to that?'

'Of course I can,' agreed Vi. 'You're my mistress and I
must do as you say—and you're my best friend, too, so I
would do it anyway. We need to make a plan.'

So, Diary, that is what we have done today. Usually after
breakfast I give Vi some lessons—I am teaching her to read
and write because she's never been to school. Today, instead
of lessons, she gathered together some of the things which I
want to save. We have found a box in which to store them.

I was very tired after that and had to rest, but when I
woke up I had a good idea. I thought it would be fun to
make a treasure hunt and hide each thing in a separate
place. Perhaps Hamish can do the treasure hunt when he is
about my age. Goodness, I might be married by then, I will
be a grown-up! Each day I will think of a place where I can
hide a treasure and make up a clue. It will be fun.

Today, looking out of the window at the river I saw
mother duck out with her six tiny ducklings. They are
so sweet and fluffy. The wild flowers are growing in the
meadow and there are yellow iris flowers in bloom on the
river bank. I do wish I could go out—I wonder sometimes
if I'll ever be able to go outside again. Vi tells me to cheer
up and hope for the best, but we both know that I'm not
getting better as quickly as I should. The doctor is coming
tomorrow to bleed me with leeches. I hate it so much when
he does that—the horrible slimy creatures sticking to my
skin and sucking my blood. How can that make me better?
However, Mama and Papa pay him a lot of money, so I
suppose it must help. I wish they would let me go to the
spa and bathe in the water, I'm sure that would be a better

cure. The other day I read in the Bible a story of Naaman who was sent to wash seven times in the river Jordan, and he was cured of leprosy. I wonder if Vi could sneak me down the back stairs to the river Wey; if I dipped seven times into it, maybe I would be cured.

Vi has promised to take you, dear Diary, to her room every night, and hide you, just in case Papa reads you and stops our secret plans!

She has also hidden treasure number one—and this is the clue:

There is a place where my diary hides,
A place near the head of Violet's bed;
It stays alone, but the brick next door
Can also move—look there instead.

So, dear Diary, keep our secret well. I may not talk to you for a few days—I always feel terrible after I have had the leeches on me.

Good night.

'Wow!' Tilly said to herself as she closed the diary and put out the light. 'This is so cool—a treasure hunt! I can't wait to tell everyone about it tomorrow.'

Tilly slept soundly that night, dreaming a funny mixed-up dream about her mum, Mab and ducklings all dipping in the river outside her window.

Tilly always checked that her brothers had made their beds properly in the mornings—she was always a bit afraid of upsetting people, and she didn't want to break Aunt Eliza's rules, even though her great-aunt wasn't half as strict as she had feared. She wondered whether to tell Toby and Alfie about the diary, but decided she would wait until breakfast, so that Aunt Eliza would hear about the treasure hunt, too.

The boys were excited and so was their great-aunt when she told them what she had read the previous night.

'I couldn't wait until this evening to tell you what I read in the diary,' she said. 'Please can we go back into the attic today?'

'Charlie and Poppy are coming this morning to start making a den,' Alfie reminded her, 'but a treasure hunt sounds so cool!'

'I have a plan,' said Aunt Eliza. 'The morning is forecast to be dry and sunny, but possibly there will be showers later in the day. Why don't you build the den this morning? If Charlie and Poppy are free this afternoon they can join you and search in the attic for the treasure. You could do a bit more tidying up there as well if you have time. My neighbours will be back in a day or so, and I'm sure they won't want five baby elephants crashing around in their roof!'

The boys cleared the dishes and stacked them in the dishwasher while Tilly had her favourite job to do: to feed the ducks. These ducks came up from the river at around the same time every morning and evening, and Aunt Eliza liked to feed them. They were used to the children now and quite tame. One of them was tapping his beak against the back door, almost asking for his breakfast! Tilly put a measure of grain into the dish and gave them some fresh water. The ducks had messed up the back step, so she got some hot water and a scrubbing brush and made it all clean again.

'I must text Faith and tell her about the ducks,' she thought to herself. 'She'll never believe that I've just scrubbed a back doorstep, either—it sounds as if I'm living in Victorian times too! She'll be jealous when I tell her about the treasure hunt.'

Faith and her family were on holiday in the South of France, but they still sent texts to each other most days. France sounded nice, and Tilly liked the photos Faith sent her, but secretly she decided they were having more fun at Aunt Eliza's house.

It was a good job that not only did Greystones have a large garden, but there were willow trees on the river bank and other sources of wood to use to build a den. It needed to be substantial as the boys were going to sleep in it. The girls didn't mind helping to get the material and build it, but they were secretly glad they were going to be sleeping in the tent! As they went about looking for branches, Tilly was glad she had abandoned her shorts for jeans, as the grass and nettles were quite high in places. They took all morning to get enough large branches and sticks to make a strong structure and began to build the den on a level piece of ground in the top field.

'We need to get some long grass and try to make a roof like the ones Africans put over their huts,' commented Charlie.

'Wherever will we find enough stuff to do that?' asked Toby.

'Down at the old mill there's a plant which looks like giant rhubarb—we could ask Mrs Dobbins, who lives there, if we could have some,' suggested Poppy.

'Why don't you and Tilly go and ask her,' suggested Charlie. 'She likes you and will probably agree. If I go, she'll just remind me how many times my football has ended up in her garden!'

The girls went to the Mill House. It took them only a couple of minutes to reach it, and they found Mrs Dobbins in her garden.

'Hello, Poppy,' she called out as they arrived at the gate. 'Are you coming to see me?'

'Yes, I am,' Poppy answered. 'This is Tilly, who's staying with her auntie at Greystones. We've come to ask if we might have some of your giant rhubarb leaves. We're making a den and need to have something large to make a roof,' she added.

'I'd heard that Miss Eliza had company. I'm pleased to meet you, Tilly,' replied Mrs Dobbins. 'So you want some Gunnera leaves? They're huge—you'll need to borrow my wheelbarrow to take them over the road. Come with me and I'll cut some down for you. It'll be good for the plant to have a pruning,' she added. 'You'll have to be careful, though, because the stems are prickly.'

Soon they had a wheelbarrow full of leaves—Tilly had never seen anything like them, they were so big! They thanked Mrs Dobbins and then carefully crossed the road, wheeling the barrow back to Greystones. It wasn't easy making a roof with the leaves as they were big and heavy, but between the five of them they managed, and the girls returned the wheelbarrow with many thanks from them all.

'You can come over and see our den, if you like,' said Poppy. 'It's looking really good!'

'Maybe I will,' Mrs Dobbins replied. 'I could call on Eliza and have a chat—I've not done that for a long time.'

'Aunt Eliza would like that, I'm sure,' Tilly told her. 'She's always got the kettle on the boil, but she does have a rest after lunch for about an hour.'

'I'm sure she needs that, looking after a family this summer!' Mrs Dobbins said with a smile.

Chapter nine

After lunch the children went up to the boys' bedroom and the five of them managed to push aside the chest of drawers to reveal the secret door to the attic. They were very excited and wanted to find the first part of the treasure.

Tilly took them to the place where she had been when she had caught her foot and discovered the secret cavity behind the brick. She couldn't remember exactly which brick had moved, but she knew it was about the third row from the floor. With all of them pushing bricks, they should find it; one of the other bricks around it must then contain the treasure and the next clue.

Alfie was delighted when he found a brick that moved, and he shone his torch into the cavity. It had nothing in it, but he could see that the dust had been disturbed, so they decided it must have been the diary's hiding place. Toby had brought a piece of chalk with him, so they marked that brick with a D.

'We may want to put the diary back,' he explained. 'If we can't work out the treasure hunt, maybe someone else will in years to come. I hope we can do it, though,' he added.

'Now we just have to see if one of the bricks next to it will move,' said Charlie. 'That shouldn't be too difficult.' He began to push at one above the cavity, and Toby one at the side, while Poppy and Tilly tried ones below.

'Got it!' shouted Poppy, beside herself with excitement, as the brick she was pushing slid away to reveal another secret cavity. She swung her torch around it and right at the back saw a little parcel.

'Take it out gently,' said Tilly. 'It's been there for over 160 years, so it may be fragile.'

Poppy put in her hand, then screamed loudly, 'There's a huge spider in there!'

'Girls!' muttered Charlie. 'Get out of the way, Poppy, I'm not scared of spiders.'

'Just be careful, don't damage the package,' reminded Tilly. 'It's old.'

'Don't fuss, I'll be careful,' Charlie muttered again, pulling out a very dusty little box.

He handed it to Tilly, who took it carefully and blew off the worst of the dust.

It was a small red (though now very faded) box, with a tiny gold-coloured clasp.

The children moved nearer to the ceiling light and Tilly gently opened the box. Inside was a folded piece of paper. Under the paper was a ring—dirty, but it looked like gold, with a tiny red stone at the centre.

'It's beautiful!' exclaimed Poppy. 'Is it "finders keepers"—is it mine?'

'I don't know—I think probably it should belong to Aunt Eliza, as it's her house,' Toby said. 'We certainly need to show her and see what she says. Let's see what's on the paper. Unfold it carefully—it might fall to pieces.'

Tilly, being the oldest and still holding the box, opened the paper and shone her torch over the faded words:

*You have found my ring. It was given to me by my
grandmamma on my tenth birthday. It is gold and
has a ruby at the centre: rubies are for compassion,
Grandmamma told me, and she said that she hoped I
would grow up with a compassionate heart.*

'What's compassion?' asked Alfie.

'I think it means loving and caring,' answered Tilly,
before continuing to read the note:

*Now you must solve the next riddle to find my second
treasure:*
    1, 2, 3, carefully as you tread,
    1, 2, 3, up you go to bed.

'Whatever can that mean?' Poppy asked. 'It doesn't
make much sense.'

'Something about going to bed. If you think you're
sleeping in Mab's room, Tilly, maybe that's the next place
to search,' suggested Toby.

'It could be, but we think Vi slept up here,' said Tilly.
'Maybe we have to count three bricks from the one where
the ring was hidden. Shall we try?'

'I can do that,' said Alfie. 'I'll try all the bricks around
the ring's hiding place. Maybe you should mark R on that
brick, so we know where we are,' he added.

'Good thinking, Alfie,' his brother said, marking the
brick with the chalk.

Alfie tapped around, and the others came to help, but
no brick moved.

'Perhaps it was near the bed where Vi slept,' said Poppy. 'We'll never find the clue—there are hundreds of bricks up here.'

Tilly shone her torch round to the place where, on the first day they had climbed up into the attic, she had thought that a window had been blocked up.

'If that was the only window in the attic room, I think Vi's bed would have been near it. Let's try around there.'

The children rushed to the other side of the attic. All of them wanted to be the one to find the next part of the treasure—especially if it did mean 'finders keepers'.

They tried pushing lots of the bricks around on both sides of the bricked-up window, but without success. They were starting to get a bit fed up, and it was so dusty in the attic that they were all quite thirsty.

'I vote we give up for now,' said Toby. 'Let's go and have a drink and play in the den. P'raps we'll get another idea later on.' They all agreed.

Tilly carefully folded up the piece of paper and put it back in the red box. She put the box into her jeans pocket and they all trooped down the tiny staircase, moving the chest of drawers back after them.

In the snug by the kitchen they found Aunt Eliza, refreshed by her nap. They told her about the ring and the riddle, and she promised to look after the ring while they went back into the garden to play.

'I'll make you a jug of juice and bring it out to you with some biscuits,' she said. 'I want to see this den of yours and see if it's fit for human habitation.'

'What does that mean?' asked Alfie.

'It means, whether I'll allow you to sleep in it or not,' Aunt Eliza said, looking stern, but with a twinkle in her eye.

Back in the garden the children tidied up the den to make it as smart as possible. The Gunnera leaves were prickly, so they found as much long grass as they could to cover them over. Aunt Eliza had told them to look in the garage for a ground sheet, which they found and put in the den to make a floor.

In the garage, they were amazed to find a beautiful red sports car. They didn't know their aunt owned a car, let alone such a fantastic model!

'Wow!' Toby exclaimed. 'That is so cool. I wonder if Dad knows it's here? He would love it!'

'You can ask him tonight when he calls us,' said Alfie. 'When he comes, maybe Aunt Eliza will let him take us out in it.'

'I wouldn't be so sure,' Tilly said. 'I think this may be *her* hidden treasure.'

'I've never seen it out on the road,' Charlie said. 'I'm sure Mum would know if she drove a car like that.'

When Aunt Eliza came out, carrying a tray with drinks and biscuits, Poppy ran down to help her. As they walked over the bridge and up to the top field, she asked about the car. Aunt Eliza went quiet for a few seconds.

'When I sent you to the garage, I forgot that the car was there,' she eventually said. 'It's a long story, and I don't really want to talk about it. It does belong to me, but it hasn't been on the road for many years.'

When they reached the den, Poppy could see the boys were going to ask about the car, so she decided to tell them what she had been told, to save the elderly lady any more embarrassment.

'I asked about the car, and Aunt Eliza hasn't driven it for many years and doesn't want to talk about it.'

The others were stunned by Poppy's announcement: it was unlike her to be so forceful, but they didn't ask any questions and Aunt Eliza gave her a very grateful smile.

'My goodness,' she said, 'you need some cushions to sit on, and I could do with a garden chair. Boys, run and get some from the shed, please.'

When they were all sitting enjoying their biscuits and sipping their drinks, Aunt Eliza began to talk about the treasure hunt.

'For now,' she said, 'I think that the ring, and any other treasures you might retrieve, should be kept together and at the end of the hunt, provided the things are still around to be found, we can decide what should happen to them.

'Meanwhile, I've been thinking about the second clue. "1, 2, 3, carefully as you tread" must mean the tread of the stairs.'

'What is a "tread"?' asked Tilly.

'It's the flat part on which you place your foot,' she told them. 'So I think we have to look at the third tread of a staircase.'

'But Auntie,' said Toby, 'which staircase? Didn't you tell us that the layout was different when Greystones was one big house? Our stairs belonged to the stables, not the house, didn't they?'

'Yes, sort of,' replied their great-aunt. 'The stairs we use went up to the rooms above the stable block, but the stairs from the first to the second floor are original, as far as I can remember. Also, behind my wardrobe on the first floor is a little door with a few stairs, and it leads into the house next door—that's why it's blocked off by my wardrobe.'

'Oh, Auntie, do you think it would be all right if we looked at those stairs?' asked Tilly. 'We wouldn't go into the house next door.'

'Well, I don't know,' relied Aunt Eliza. 'I don't know if we could even move the wardrobe—it's heavier than the chest of drawers we moved before, and that was a struggle. I would have to be with you: I have to be responsible to my neighbours.'

'Wow—this is so cool!' said Tilly. 'It really is like the Narnia stories—a hidden door behind a wardrobe! We must try—please let us try! With Charlie and Poppy and all of us, surely we could do it!'

'I really don't know,' said Aunt Eliza hesitantly.

'Maybe if we waited until our dad got home, he could help us?' suggested Charlie. 'He'll be home soon after 5 p.m.'

'That would be the best plan, if he doesn't mind,' answered Aunt Eliza. 'We'll just have one try at those stairs. If we find nothing, there's no going back, do you understand that?'

After their drinks, the children played rounders in the field, and the time passed very quickly. As soon as it was five o'clock, Poppy and Charlie raced home so they could ask their dad to help move the wardrobe the moment he came in from work.

Even Aunt Eliza seemed excited when he arrived at Greystones, toolbox in hand. He and the boys managed to move the wardrobe without too much difficulty, and there behind it was the door.

Toby tried the handle, but it wouldn't move.

'It must be locked,' he said with disappointment.

'I'm sure I've got a key somewhere,' Aunt Eliza said, rummaging through one of her dressing table drawers. 'Here it is!' she said triumphantly, holding it out to Toby.

'I still can't open it,' said Toby after he'd tried it. 'The key fits, but it won't turn.'

'Ah, I guess it needs a little oil,' Charlie's dad remarked, and he got out a spray can from his toolbox. 'This'll do the trick.'

The door groaned as it opened, almost telling everyone that it hadn't been opened for years and years. There were three stairs leading up to another door.

'We can't all go up those stairs at once, there isn't room,' said Aunt Eliza. 'So I suggest Charlie and his father go and look at the third stair.'

They were old, wooden stairs with no carpet, so it was easy for Charlie's dad to gently prise open the top stair. Charlie shone his torch inside. There was quite a large hole, and inside was an oblong-shaped package.

'Handle it carefully, son,' said his dad, 'it looks as if the paper around it may crumble to dust.'

Charlie took the package into Aunt Eliza's bedroom. The others gathered round to see what he had found, while his father carefully nailed the tread back into place and then came down, relocking the door.

'Let's take this down to the kitchen and open it there, once we've put the wardrobe back in place,' Charlie's dad instructed them. The boys went at once to help, and then they all traipsed down to the kitchen. It was the best place, as the paper around the 'treasure' was falling to pieces and very dirty.

Even the adults were excited as Charlie carefully took off the paper and they all saw an exquisitely carved ivory box. Inside was a message from Mab:

This is my pencil box. It was given to me by my Uncle Augustus when he returned from an expedition to China. I hope that whoever finds it will treasure it and enjoy using it.

'Wow! It's really beautiful!' said Toby. 'Look at the carving—it's far too good to use for pencils!'

'I agree,' Aunt Eliza said, 'and these days, old ivory carvings are worth a lot of money. I've seen that on the antiques shows on TV—especially if they come from China. We'll keep it in a safe place along with the ring for the time being.'

'Isn't there another piece of paper with the next clue on it?' asked Tilly. 'There must be one somewhere.'

They looked inside the box and at first couldn't see anything, but then they noticed that a piece of paper was lining the box, so neatly that it looked part of it. They eased it out and gently unfolded it:

The yaffle lives in my favourite tree;
Perch on the branch and you will see.

Chapter ten

'I wish I had my tablet and we could get on the Internet,' said Toby grumpily. 'I could google that funny word and find out what it means. This clue is so hard—it could take us weeks to work it out! Anyway, there are hundreds of trees around here—we don't have any idea which one would have been her favourite.'

'I suggest you just sleep on it and try to work out the clue tomorrow,' said Aunt Eliza. 'I need to get dinner on the table. Will you come and help me, Tilly? Toby and Alfie can feed the ducks. Your father will be on the phone to you soon, so we need to be ready.

'And thank you so much for your help,' she added, looking at Charlie and Poppy's dad. 'I guess we'll see you tomorrow.'

'We've got relatives coming for the day,' he said, 'but I'll come over with Poppy and Charlie after they've gone home and make sure they can get the tent up and all is good for the sleepover in the field. Say goodbye, kids, then we'll be off for our meal.'

The children scattered and each of them started to try to work out the clue. Even Aunt Eliza was struggling to remember what a 'yaffle' was—somewhere deep within her mind she knew she had heard the word before, but for the life of her, she couldn't recall the meaning. That was the trouble with getting older, she thought to herself: it was so hard to remember names.

They had just finished clearing away the dishes after their meal when Tilly's phone began to ring. They all rushed to listen to the news about their mum, and for a few minutes forgot all about the treasure hunt.

'Hi, family,' said their dad in a much more cheerful voice than usual. 'God is answering our prayers—Mummy has woken up properly today! She is speaking, although it's hard for her to say words properly. She asked about you all and sends her love.

'I had a long talk with the doctor who's looking after her and he feels sure that she'll learn to use her leg and arm again, which are paralysed still, but it will take a long time for her to recover completely. Some of the tubes have been taken away now and she's being transferred from Intensive Care to a High Dependency ward. If she settles down well, I can collect you and bring you home for a couple of nights, so you can visit her. If you hand the phone over to Aunt Eliza I'll arrange it with her.'

The children were delighted and very excited at the prospect of being able to visit their mum in the hospital. Tilly found she was crying—not from sadness but relief, because deep down she had been afraid that her mum might never walk or talk again.

Their dad arranged with Aunt Eliza that he would collect them on Monday afternoon and bring them back on Wednesday morning.

'Instead of us praying in my bedroom tonight, why don't we stay in the snug and then Auntie can join us to say thank you to Jesus for helping Mum?' suggested Tilly.

The children sat on cushions on the floor in the snug and Aunt Eliza in her favourite armchair. She felt strangely moved that the children wanted to have her with them while they prayed, but she hardly knew what to do or say. She wasn't used to talking to God, but she felt she couldn't let them down. As the children prayed one by one, just saying their 'thank you's in a heartfelt but simple way, she gained courage and said a little prayer out loud, realizing that she didn't need special language but could just say thank you as the children did. At the end of her prayer she also said thank you to God for bringing the children to stay with her and for the fun they were having together.

When they had all said 'amen' and looked up, they saw their great-aunt wiping a tear from her eye.

'Up to bed with you all!' she said quickly, embarrassed at her emotions. 'Sleep tight, and mind the bugs don't bite!'—remembering what her nanny used to say to her when she was very small.

Once in her bed, Tilly opened the diary again.

'Dear Diary,' she read,

I am sorry that I have neglected you for so long now. I felt so weak after the doctor bled me—I'm sure it does no good, maybe even harm, but Papa says that is rubbish and I have one of the best doctors in the county. Lately Papa has been bringing up a cup of the spa water each evening for me to drink, hoping that it might help to cure me. It tastes horrible and makes me feel sick, but I drink it to make him happy.

Most of the time I stay in bed now. My legs are too weak for me to walk and I have no breath. Papa says my heart is very weak and I mustn't strain it, but yesterday I had a

*very special treat. He carried me into the playroom at the
front of the house and Mama was outside and I could look
down and see Hamish—he's such a tiny baby, but so sweet!
He was wrapped up in a shawl—I wish I could have seen
his tiny hands and feet—but I am so glad that I have seen
my brother at last.*

*Vi is such fun, always cheerful, even on my bad days
when I feel cross and irritable because I am confined to
bed. I gave her my best doll and she has taken it to the
attic. She has never had a doll and although she is older
than me, I can see she loves it. I think she is missing her
little brothers and sisters, too, but I'm so glad she is living
here now. I don't always feel well enough to play games
with her or to give her reading and writing lessons as I
used to, but I do try sometimes, and we had lessons today.
She is so clever and learns quickly. Her brother Sidney,
the groom, helps with the horses and is living above the
stables, so she does get some other company. She ought to
have her half-day off each week to go and see her family,
but she won't take it because she's afraid she might take
germs to the little ones. Neither of us talk about it, but we
both know that I am not going to get better. I do talk to
Jesus about going to live with Him in heaven—and I pray
that I will be ready when the time comes.*

*My bed is near the window and I love to look out over
the river and see the ducks. Sometimes I see the otters
playing on the bank, or just catch a glimpse of a silvery
head as one swims by. At least I have the river to look at
now that I can no longer sit up in the apple tree and watch
the world go by. I wonder how many children have sat in
that tree and how many more will do so?*

I'm tired now, so must try to sleep. Goodnight, my diary friend.

Tilly put the book down and turned off the light. She found herself thinking about Mab. What must it have been like to have been left up in these rooms for weeks on end, seeing so few people and growing weaker and weaker? What must it have been like to know you were slowly dying? It was so frightening. She tried to put herself in Mab's place: would she be ready to go to heaven? How did she know that she would actually go there, and not to the other place—hell? She shuddered as she thought about that.

Not long before the sports day when she had become so ill, her mum had been baptized at 'Sausage Church'. Tilly hadn't really understood what it was all about, but her mum had explained that she had asked Jesus to forgive all the wrong things she had ever said or done, and that being baptized was like showing other people she had been washed clean inside by Jesus and was now a new person, loved Him and would put Him first in her life. Tilly knew she believed in God—she talked to Him most days—but she also knew there were lots of things in her life she had done wrong and of which she was ashamed. She often told lies—just silly little ones—and she could be mean to her brothers, and . . .

As she thought of many of the things she wished she hadn't said or done, she began to cry. She realized she wasn't the nice person people often thought she was. Inside, she was often horrible.

'I'm so sorry, Jesus,' she sobbed. 'Please will You forgive me and help me to love You. And when it's my time to die—and I hope I'll be very old—but whenever it happens, please may I come to live with you in heaven.'

After praying this prayer, which Tilly meant with all her heart, she felt peaceful and strangely clean inside. She drifted into sleep and dreamt about apple trees. She was sitting in one, quite high up and looking out over the river. She could hear a 'tap, tap, tap', and she saw that above her a green woodpecker was making a hole in the tree.

When she awoke in the morning, the sun was streaming through the window. She looked down at the river wondering if there were still otters in the river—and then she remembered her dream.

'The apple tree must have been Mab's favourite tree,' she realized, 'and perhaps the woodpecker is the yaffle.'

With that, she leapt out of bed, got washed and dressed and ran down to find her great-aunt.

'Auntie,' she said, her eyes shining with excitement, 'is a yaffle a green woodpecker?'

'Yes! That's what it is!' said Aunt Eliza. 'I knew I'd heard the word before; I'd been racking my brains to remember what it meant! How did you discover its meaning?'

Tilly told her about the part of the diary she had read the previous night and then the dream of the woodpecker in the apple tree.

'I want to rush out and climb the tree—but then I thought that Alfie should try to look for the answer to the clue; he's really cool at climbing trees, and he'd be excited to find something.'

'That's a kind thought,' replied Aunt Eliza. 'The boys should be down for breakfast at any moment. But don't tell him until after you've eaten, otherwise he'll rush out straight away.'

Sure enough, as soon as Alfie was told about the clue in the apple tree, he rushed outside. In no time at all he had shinned up the tree and begun to look for the hole made by the woodpecker. He soon found it and was just about to try to get his hand into it when he heard Toby call him.

'Wait, Alfie,' Toby told him. 'Please wait until the others come this evening. We ought to do this together.'

But as Alfie turned around, he lost his balance and fell. With a scream he landed on the ground. Aunt Eliza and Tilly rushed over to him.

'Are you all right, Alfie?' they both asked, and Toby was almost in tears, kneeling beside his younger brother.

'I think so,' Alfie answered, 'but my knee's bleeding a bit.'

When Aunt Eliza was sure that Alfie was not concussed and hadn't broken any bones, she took him inside, washed the cut and bandaged it.

'I think you'd better wait until this evening before climbing that old tree again,' she said. 'Why don't you all make some get well cards for your mother to take with you when you visit?'

The children thought this was a great idea so they spent the morning making cards and writing letters to tell their mum about all their adventures.

Chapter eleven

Later in the day Charlie, Poppy and their father arrived to put up the tent and make the den ready with sleeping bags for the sleepover. Then they went searching around for sticks to make a camp fire and cook sausages for their evening meal. They had their dog, Spot, as well, and had a hard job trying to keep him away from the sausages as they cooked them. The children also ate jacket potatoes, which had been wrapped in foil and baked in the red-hot embers. It all tasted delicious—far nicer than sausages and potatoes would ever have tasted indoors!

Afterwards, as it was still light, Alfie asked if he could climb the tree again and try to get the clue. This time he was careful and managed to put his hand into the hole in the tree. At first, all he could find were soggy old leaves and bits of an old bird's nest. He was feeling very disappointed and about to give up the search when his fingers came across something hard. It was a small box. Once he had managed to pull it out and scrape away all the muck which had settled on it, he saw that it had a small clasp. He handed it down to Poppy and climbed carefully back down the tree. His knee still hurt a little, but he didn't want to make a fuss in case Aunt Eliza stopped him from sleeping in the den.

'Can I open it?' asked Poppy.

'No, it should be Alfie, since he found the clue,' Charlie answered. So Poppy handed the box back to Alfie once he was safely on the ground, but as he tried to open the box, it fell to pieces. Inside was a brooch. It didn't look very exciting—it was very dirty—but tucked under the pin was the next clue.

'I think we need to take this inside and look at it very carefully,' Tilly said. 'It's old and very fragile.'

Inside, on the kitchen table Tilly gently extracted the piece of paper and unfolded it. It was hard to make out the words, so Aunt Eliza went to her cupboard and found a magnifying glass. It helped and they were able to just make out the writing:

Not guarded by a troll,
Walk four paces and dig a hole.

'Write it down on a clean piece of paper, Toby,' suggested Tilly. 'Then we can remember it exactly and try to work it out.'

'This is a beautiful brooch,' remarked Aunt Eliza, who had taken a soft cloth and was gently cleaning it. 'It's a cameo, and I think it may be gold.'

'What's a cameo?' asked Poppy, going over to look at the piece of treasure.

'It's a little picture of someone. Maybe this was Mabel's mother or grandmother. It's been carved in a gemstone—I think it may be carved in onyx, a semi-precious stone. It's so beautifully done. Look, there's a little mark on the pin: I think it's a jeweller's hallmark, so it must be gold.'

Everyone came over to look, and then they put it together with the other treasures they had found.

It was hard to go to bed after all the excitement of the find, but Charlie and Poppy's dad wanted to see they were all safely in the tent and the den before he went home. He left Spot, their dog, to guard them, and although it was still quite light he made sure that they had torches under their pillows. The children didn't know it, but he planned to come and sleep in the snug, so that the back door could be left open in case anyone should need to use the toilet in the night. He knew that Aunt Eliza would sleep more soundly knowing he was there.

The boys in the den and the girls in the tent talked about the next clue. None of them had any idea what it meant. They were just settling to sleep when Spot began to bark and they heard noises coming from the river. The girls scrambled out of their sleeping bags and went to the den, only to find that boys had already done the same.

'Something's happening on the river,' said Toby. 'We're going to see what's up.'

They ran through the little gate near the house which led to some steps down to the river, flashing their torches around to see what might be happening. Spot was with them, barking loudly.

'Look, there's a little dog caught in some weeds, almost drowning!' yelled Charlie. 'We must rescue it.'

The current was flowing fast, due to the recent rain, and the poor little animal couldn't get free. Toby and Charlie waded into the river and between them managed to free the dog and carry him back to the bank. He was only a puppy and was very scared and cold. He even tried to bite Toby in his fear.

'We need a towel to dry him. I'll get the one from the downstairs loo,' said Tilly, running back into the house. When she went through the door and saw a man in the shadows, she let out a huge scream, not realizing it was her friends' father. All of this woke up Aunt Eliza, who soon appeared in her bedroom slippers and fluffy dressing gown.

In a few minutes Tilly had explained everything and the grown-ups helped by bringing more towels and a blanket. The little puppy had water weed caught in its mouth which the boys managed to extract; then it began to breathe more freely. Charlie and Poppy's dad decided he would keep the puppy near him in the snug for the night; they could decide how to look for its owner in the morning. Meanwhile, the boys had to get showered and put on clean pyjamas—it was a good job Toby had some spare ones to lend Charlie! Aunt Eliza then decided that everyone needed a midnight feast of biscuits and hot chocolate before going back to bed.

'That's a really cool idea!' said Poppy. 'I've always wanted a midnight feast!'

They all sat on the floor in the snug and enjoyed the feast before finally going back to the tent and den for the night. This time they fell asleep quickly, for it truly was past midnight.

The next morning, since it was Sunday, breakfast was a little later, and that was just as well as everyone was tired after all the midnight adventures and sleeping in strange places! Charlie and Poppy went home with their dad and Spot, and Tilly, Toby and Alfie showered and dressed tidily, ready to visit St Ann's Church in Radipole with their great-aunt. The puppy seemed to be fine, so they left him in the back porch with food and water while they went out.

It was quite a long walk to the church, but Aunt Eliza managed it, and it was lovely and cool inside the building. Parts of the church were ancient, and Tilly thought she would like to explore it sometime. Although they were the only children in the congregation and found it difficult to follow the service in the prayer books they had been given, everyone was friendly, and they sang the songs as best they could. Afterwards, they crossed the road to the old school for refreshments. Even after a hearty breakfast they enjoyed the biscuits and squash, while Aunt Eliza drank a cup of tea and chatted. It had been years since she had last attended the church and she had been very moved by the service. When the church warden found out who the family were and that their ancestors were buried in the churchyard and had memorials on the walls of the church, she took the children to see them, while their great-aunt continued to chat. It was amazing to think that many generations of their grandfathers and grandmothers had belonged to the same church and had prayed in it hundreds of years before!

Aunt Eliza discovered a friend in the church, who offered to drive her home, but the children decided they would like to walk. As they walked they chatted together and tried to work out the next clue in the treasure hunt.

Suddenly, Alfie remembered a story book they had all read when they were small—*Grimm's Fairy Tales*, it was called.

'Do you remember the story of the troll who guarded the bridge and wouldn't let anyone across?' he asked the others.

'Oh yes! Well done, Alfie—I think you've solved the clue!' said Toby. 'It must mean that little bridge over the ditch between the garden and the field. We'll have to walk four paces and dig. I wonder what we'll find this time?'

They hoped to dig that afternoon, but Aunt Eliza had other ideas.

'We must try and find out if anyone has lost a puppy,' she announced. 'You need to write some notices and stick them on the lampposts and telegraph poles in the village asking if anyone has lost him. Then you need to pack a few things to take home, because tomorrow you're going back to see your mother. You must all have a hair-wash and look good for her, too. I don't want her to think I'm not taking good care of you!'

Chapter twelve

It was great to see Dad again, and to be back home for a couple of nights. They all wanted to tell their father about the adventures they were having and their new friends, Poppy and Charlie.

Tilly had taken the diary with her, hoping to read a bit more, but she also wanted to use the computer and email Faith, who was still on holiday with her family. The boys wanted to play on the Xbox and use their tablets, and in the evening the family watched a Disney film together. It did seem strange without their mum, and Tilly tried to take her place by helping to cook supper and making sure the kitchen was tidy.

At the end of the day they phoned Aunt Eliza. This was the children's idea, and she was delighted to hear them.

'I took the puppy to the vet and he checked it over,' she told them. 'It doesn't have a tag, whatever that means, so he can't trace any owner. He thinks he's about six months old, and he said we can look after him until he is claimed. If no one comes for him, I will need to decide whether or not to keep him. The vet says he's a mongrel but thinks he will be quite a small dog. I think I shall call him Heinz, as he may have a variety of breeds in his genetic make-up. Your father can explain that. I'm having a lazy day today and missing you,' she added.

'We're missing you too, Auntie. We'll phone you tomorrow and see you on Wednesday. Love you!' they shouted down the phone.

Their father was laughing. 'You seem to be loving Aunt Eliza and cracking the hard shell she had around her heart!'

'We love her to bits!' answered Toby. 'She's really fun when you get to know her, and her rules are sensible— she's not as strict as she looks. Did you know she has a fantastic red Alfa Romeo sports car in her garage?'

'Yes, but there's a sad story behind that which is hers to tell you if she wants to, not mine. Don't ask her—she'll tell you if she wants you to know.'

'So why has she chosen the name Heinz?' asked Alfie, still thinking about the puppy and glad Aunt Eliza could keep him for now.

'Go and get the bottle of Heinz Tomato Ketchup from the fridge,' instructed his dad, so Alfie ran off and found it.

'Now read what it says on the label,' David told his son, and Alfie read out, '57 varieties.'

'That's why she's called the puppy Heinz,' their dad explained. 'He could have 57 varieties of different breeds in him! That's what being a "mongrel" means.' Then all three children began to laugh at the joke.

At bedtime the family prayed together, and their dad tried to prepare them for the changes they would see in their mother the next day, and reassure them that she would get better, although only very slowly. He then sent them up to bed.

When he came up to hug and kiss them goodnight, Tilly took the opportunity to ask him about something which was on her mind.

'Dad, while I've been at Auntie's, I've been reading this diary, which started us all on the treasure hunt. When I read about Mab being so ill and sort of getting ready to die, it made me think. I thought about Mum and how she was baptized not long ago, and I asked Jesus to be my friend and forgive me for the wrong things I've said and done. Since then, things have been different inside me—I can't explain it, but I know they are and that I love Jesus now. Please, when we're properly back home, can I be baptized too?'

Tilly's dad was silent for a moment before he answered.

'We'll check with the minister at "Sausage Church", but I'm sure he'll be thrilled about it. I myself have promised Jesus that as soon as Mum is well enough to come back home and see it, I will get baptized, too. We could be baptized together—she would love that!' he added.

'That would be so cool!' Tilly said, giving her dad a huge hug.

Then she settled down to read a little more of the diary before she went to sleep:

Dear Diary, you have really become my friend and so, even though I do feel weak and tired, I want to tell you a few things. Today I had to stay in bed all day. I kept coughing and coughing, and each time I was coughing up fresh blood. I know what that means—I do have consumption. That is the reason why they are keeping baby Hamish away from me, and I understand. Papa and Mama don't want to lose both of their children. Mama came to see me this afternoon for a little while. She looks so tired and worried and didn't kiss me. She has made me a beautiful white nightdress with lovely embroidery all around the neck and hem. It must have taken her ages to do, with every flower stitched with her love. She hates me being stuck up here on the nursery floor just as much as I am tired of staying here—but they cannot send me to Switzerland or even to a sanitorium because it would cost so much money and they must stay and run the boarding house and the spa. I think I am too ill now to get better. Vi is so good and has been finishing the treasure hunt—her brother Sidney helped her hide the clue over the bridge. I wonder who will find the treasures? Will it be Hamish when he is older? Maybe it will be children who live in a different age. I hope they have fun and enjoy my treasures.

I must write one more thing before I sleep. I cried so much last time the doctor came to bleed me that Papa told him he was not to do it again, I was losing enough blood through coughing. I am so glad! I won't have to dread his visits any more. I prayed that they would stop, and God has answered my prayers. Goodnight, dear Diary.

The next day was bright and sunny, and Tilly made sure that her brothers looked clean and tidy before they went to the hospital. The hospital was huge and seemed so busy, with doctors and nurses everywhere. There was a strange sort of disinfectant smell that seemed to be everywhere— in the corridors and the lift as well as in the ward.

They were all a bit scared, and when they went into the ward where their mum was, they were shy and found it hard to talk to her at first. She was in a room on her own. She didn't look the same: her mouth was a little twisted and she was thin and pale. She tried to reach out to them and smile and say a few words, but they could see how hard it was for her.

Then it was as if someone whispered into Tilly's head: she knew what she should do. She squeezed her mum's hand gently and began to tell her all about the diary and the treasure hunt. Soon the boys were joining in, and it didn't matter that Mum wasn't answering—they could see her trying to smile at them. Tilly also told her mum that Aunt Eliza was very kind to them and they were having a happy holiday, although they missed her very much.

'We all pray together every night and ask Jesus to make you strong and help you to walk and talk again, and we can't wait to be back home with you.'

It was just what their mother needed to hear: she didn't have to worry about them, they were happy and well cared for, but they were still missing her!

The visit made their mum tired so they couldn't stay very long, but they were so happy to see her, and she was thrilled with the cards they had made. A kind nurse stuck them up with Blu-Tack on the back of her door. Their mum tried to kiss them all and wave as they left the room, with tears in her eyes but a smile on her face.

David had taken time off work to spend with his family, so after visiting the hospital he took them to a Chinese restaurant as a treat, and then they went shopping as Alfie needed a new pair of trainers. David gave them all some pocket money to spend and was touched and proud when they decided to each contribute a little money to get a present for Aunt Eliza. They chose a silky red scarf for her and carefully wrapped it in tissue paper, adding a tag on which Tilly wrote, 'With love from Tilly, Toby and Alfie.'

While they were out shopping they also visited the pet shop, buying a collar, lead and a metal tag with the name Heinz, as well as some dog food and treats. That had been their dad's idea. He had explained what the vet meant about 'tagging' and said he would pay for the puppy to be electronically tagged if no one claimed him.

It was hard to leave their home again so soon, but the children were also wanting to get back to their great-aunt and Poppy and Charlie, to tell them they had worked out the next clue of the treasure hunt. They arrived back Wednesday lunchtime and Aunt Eliza was waiting for them. A very excited little Heinz greeted them, too—and they had to laugh at him. He wasn't very impressed when they put a collar round his neck and introduced him to a lead, but Aunt Eliza was very pleased, and she loved her scarf, too.

Chapter thirteen

Tilly sent a text to Charlie as soon as their dad left to drive back to the hospital. She was a bit disappointed to find that he and his family had gone for a picnic at Sandsfoot Castle. It was too far for them to walk and join their friends and it would mean two buses and a walk if they went by public transport, so the children had to content themselves with playing in the garden. As it was hot, they asked if they could paddle and swim in the river.

'I'll sit with Heinz under the apple tree,' Aunt Eliza told them. 'I don't want him falling into the river again. If you could clear away some of the water weed, that would be a real help,' she added.

It was great fun in the river; Toby couldn't think why they hadn't asked to play there before. It wasn't very deep but it was fast flowing. The cows in the field on the other side of the river wandered over to see what was happening. A man who was exercising his dog also came over and watched them having fun. Toby asked him if he knew of anyone who had lost a puppy, and told him about Heinz. Secretly, the children were all pleased when the man said he lived on the other side of the field and knew almost all the dog owners, but nobody had a puppy or, to his knowledge, had lost their dog.

They found some small fish in the river, but nothing large enough to catch. Alfie was sure that he saw an otter, but it turned out to be a tennis ball floating downstream.

Tilly and Toby laughed, but admitted that it did look a bit like an animal's head as it floated by.

They cleared a lot of the weed and left it on the river bank to dry out and rot down. It was much easier to swim when the weed had been cleared, so they swam downstream the length of the cottages and back. After they had showered and dressed again, Aunt Eliza surprised them by bringing out a plate of doughnuts and cold drinks.

'I thought you didn't believe in sweet things like doughnuts,' Alfie said without thinking.

'I don't usually,' Aunt Eliza said quite severely. 'They are bad for your teeth and make you fat, but occasionally it's good to have a treat. I went shopping yesterday and thought they looked rather nice. I haven't eaten one for years, and I must admit, it's gorgeous to bite into all the sugary crust and find the jam inside!'

'You're so cool, Aunt Eliza!' said Toby. 'Thank you for the treat.'

Aunt Eliza laughed. 'I don't think "cool" is the right adjective for me just now! I feel like a roasted beetroot—and I'm sure the doughnut will make my waistline get even bigger, but it *was* nice!'

'You've changed, Aunt Eliza,' said Alfie, although Tilly tried to shush him up and tell him he was being rude.

'Having you to stay is doing me a world of good,' Aunt Eliza said. 'I've never had much to do with children before, except for your father coming to stay occasionally. Once, I dreamt of having a family of my own, but it wasn't meant to be.' She sighed deeply.

'What happened, Auntie?' asked Tilly softly. 'Is it a secret or can you tell us? We'll understand if you don't want to.'

Aunt Eliza sighed again. She looked at the three children and wondered if she could tell them part of her life story. Could she trust them? They were only children—could she ask them not to talk of her secret to anyone else apart from their parents? It would be a huge risk, for she had been a very private person for many years, but these three children had already changed her life in so many ways and she loved them for it.

'I will tell you—though it may not be easy for me and I do want you to promise me that you will only talk about it with your parents: not anyone else, not even your friends like Charlie and Poppy.'

The children looked at each other and nodded. 'We promise, Auntie,' Tilly said, speaking for all three of them.

'Well, when I was in my late twenties, you wouldn't believe it but I was slim and pretty! I had lots of boyfriends, but none of them were serious relationships because I didn't want to settle down and get married. In those days, marriage usually meant that a girl had to give up her career, and I wasn't ready to do that. I worked in London as a secretary in the secret service—now known as MI5. Through my work I met all sorts of people—some were spies and even double agents! As a secretary I worked in the offices, so it wasn't always a glamorous job, but the people we met and for whom we wrote reports did dangerous and exciting things.

'One day, I met Jacob. He worked "out in the field"—not exactly a James Bond, but not far off! He was the tall, dark, handsome man every girl has dreams of marrying! He was always polite and chatted to all the girls in the office when he came in. He used to sit on the edge of my desk and tease me, calling me Eliza Jane. When he asked me to go to a dance with him one Saturday night, I was beside myself with excitement. I went out and bought a bright red dress and some red high heels, and I thought I was the bee's knees.

'We dated several times and I fell head over heels in love with him. He was a real gentleman and treated me like a queen! I remember taking him home to meet my parents—everything was very formal in those days—and he asked my father if he could court and marry me. My father seemed to like him and gave his permission, but my mother wasn't so sure. He was so glamourous that she felt he might be a heart-breaker.

'We got engaged about six months later, and as well as a ring he bought me a red Alfa Romeo racing car. He taught me to drive, and once I'd passed my test I drove all around the countryside—usually with Jacob at my side.'

'Is that the car in the garage?' asked Toby. 'It's so cool!'

'Yes, it is. I like to keep it polished, but I no longer drive it. It's like a cherished memory—rather like the treasures we're finding which Mab had hidden. I guess I've hidden it away.'

'Why, Auntie?' asked Tilly. 'What happened?'

'Well, I told you that Jacob worked for MI5. In fact—and I didn't know this to begin with—he was a double agent!'

'What does that mean?' asked Alfie.

'It means that he was working for both the British government and the government of another country. It's very dangerous work, and no one side can fully trust such an agent—and I found that I couldn't fully trust Jacob as a man. On one mission in the Soviet Union—that's what Russia used to be called—he had to befriend a beautiful lady in order to get information—or so he told me; but he

betrayed me and our engagement by living with her as
his wife. I was madly in love with him and planning our
wedding, but I knew it would never work—I could never
trust him again. Eventually he disappeared back to the
Soviet Union and didn't ever return to this country.

'I was heartbroken—and I determined that I would
never trust men or marry anyone. Very few people know
why the car is in the garage—it's a memory of a happy
time, but it all turned sour. I even ran away from God and
blamed Him for my unhappiness and loneliness—though
now I know I chose to be bitter and angry. You children
have made my life full and happy again, so I hope you will
often come and stay with your great-aunt in your school
holidays, even when your mother is better.'

For a few minutes the children were quiet—it was such
a sad story to take in. No wonder their great-aunt had
tried to put a hard shell around her heart: she had been so
badly treated.

Then Tilly spoke for them all. 'Thank you, Aunt Eliza,'
she said quietly. 'Thank you for sharing your story. It
must have been so horrible for you to be treated like that.
We love being with you. Although we do miss Mum and
Dad, we couldn't be with anyone nicer, and we'll come
again as often as we can in the holidays.'

'And we'll keep your secret about the red car,' added
Toby. 'We won't tell anyone.'

'Thank you, dears,' their great-aunt replied. 'You can talk
about this with your parents, but I would rather that everyone
in the village didn't know. One day, I may get rid of the car—
and then I will know that my heart is healed completely.'

Chapter fourteen

The next morning Poppy and Charlie came over after breakfast. It was already warm, so the gang decided that they must try to dig up the treasure before it got any hotter. Aunt Eliza wasn't at all fazed when they asked for spades to dig the ground as directed by the last clue.

'Your great-aunt is amazing!' said Charlie, dragging a large spade over the bridge—which they had decided to name 'the troll bridge'. 'Our mum would have gone nuts if we'd asked to dig up our lawn!'

'Yeah, she's really cool, isn't she?' remarked Toby. 'I didn't realize that old people could be so cool and so much fun to stay with. She's as excited about the treasure hunt as we are!'

Once they were over the troll bridge they had a discussion as to how big a 'pace' was.

'"Walk four paces" the clue says,' said Tilly. 'I wonder how long Vi's legs were? We don't want to be digging up the field in lots of different places.'

'If the treasure is metal or had been put into a tin or something,' Poppy said, 'we could ask Mrs Morris, in the last cottage before the Spa House, as she has a metal detector. She goes down to the beach in the evenings when all the people have gone home, and you wouldn't believe how much stuff she finds!'

'Do you think she would let us borrow it?' asked Alfie.

'I don't know, but if your great-aunt asked her, she probably would.'

That sounded like a good idea, so the children ran back to the house and talked to Aunt Eliza, who was trying to teach Heinz the command to sit.

'Let's go together,' Aunt Eliza suggested to the children. 'Let's put Heinz on his lead and walk him to the end of the road. Then you can stay on the bridge over the river while I explain the situation to Mrs Morris.'

Heinz still didn't like being on a lead and it took Tilly several minutes to settle him and try to get him to walk to heel down the small lane past the cottages which had once all been part of the house where Mab had lived. It must have been huge, thought Tilly; I wonder how many guests they had coming to bathe in the river Wey and drink the waters? She looked back at the row of houses and tried to see how they would have looked when it was the boarding house. It was difficult to imagine Aunt Eliza's house as a stable block! At the end of the cottages the river went under a bridge and around the spa, then under yet another bridge as it was crossed by the road, and continued to Radipole village. It seemed a long way to Tilly, but she knew it was the shortest river in England, and that made it quite special. Weymouth got its name because that was where the river entered the sea.

The children waited outside the cottage while Aunt Eliza went in and spoke to Mrs Morris. When Mrs Morris heard the story, she was happy for the children to use the detector, but decided to come with them to show them how to use it.

It was decided that Tilly's legs might be about the same length as Vi's had been, so she walked four paces and then they used the metal detector under Mrs Morris's supervision. At first nothing happened, so they moved it a little nearer the bridge—and then it began to buzz! Excitement also buzzed through the group as the boys began to dig a hole. How hard and dry the ground was! They began to sweat and took it in turns to have a go at digging. After a while, Tilly went to get everyone some water to drink and they all had a rest. While they rested, Heinz decided that digging holes might be fun and he scratched away, spraying dirt everywhere!

When the boys got going again, it was Toby who struck something hard. Afraid of damaging whatever it might be, he took a small trowel and gently eased away the earth from what seemed to be a metal box. Of course, it was very rusty and dirty, but it looked intact. He pulled it out and cleaned off as much dirt as he could.

'Let's go under the apple tree and try to open it,' Aunt Eliza said. 'It'll be cooler there.'

Mrs Morris wanted to stay and see what they had found. She was fascinated by the story of the diary and the treasure hunt.

'Why can't I get it to open?' exclaimed Toby in frustration, as he struggled to open the lid.

'Let me have a go,' said Mrs Morris. 'Sometimes I use my pocket knife to prise off lids when I find tins on the beach.'

She was far more patient and her experience paid off. She gently eased off the lid and handed the tin back to Toby. They all tried to get near and see what was inside.

'It looks like a thin metal stick,' said Alfie in disappointment. 'I thought it would be something exciting.'

'It must be exciting because Mab wanted to hide it,' said Poppy. 'Maybe if we rub away the dirt we'll see better.'

Tilly produced a tissue and spat on it, then Toby used it to rub the stick. 'I wonder if it's magic and, like Aladdin's lamp, it will produce a genie!' Alfie said. A grin spread over everyone's face.

'I don't know,' said Aunt Eliza, 'what with trolls and genies—we're in a world of make-believe, like Alice in Wonderland! We'll see a Mad Hatter next!'

'I don't know about that, but your dog is going mad digging that hole!' Mrs Morris remarked. 'We'd better fill it in as soon as this is dealt with.'

'Look,' said Toby, 'I think it's a silver propelling pencil. Granddad used to have one in his study.'

'Let me see,' said Aunt Eliza, and as she took it everyone crowded round. 'You're right, I think it is silver. We'll clean it up and put it with the other treasures.'

'What about the next clue?' asked Poppy. 'There must be one in the tin.'

The tin was rusty, but carefully folded at the bottom was some paper. Poppy gently pulled it out and unfolded it. Inside was a second piece of paper, and this had the clue. She unfolded that and Aunt Eliza went to get her magnifying glass to make it easier to read the faded writing:

These are treasures from the sea,
You can pick them up for free,

But the pelican keeps them safe for me.
Remember well the rhyme which says,
'What a wonderful bird is the pelican . . .'

The children puzzled over the clue for a few minutes.
'You only get pelicans in the zoo, so it doesn't make any
sense,' said Alfie.

'No, it has to mean somewhere around here,' Charlie
said. 'We're missing something.'

Aunt Eliza smiled, letting them think. She knew
exactly where the pelicans were but kept quiet because
she wanted them to work out the clue for themselves.

'Just walk around the house, inside and out, to look for
pelicans, while I get your lunch ready,' she said. 'Charlie,
Poppy, is your mother expecting you home for lunch, or
would you like to stay? I thought a picnic in the den might
be fun,' she suggested.

'I'll just text Mum and see if we can stay—a picnic
sounds cool,' answered Charlie as he got out his phone and
started to text.

Then the children went from room to room looking for
anything which might resemble a pelican. After searching
inside they began the tour outside. It was hot, and they
were starting to get a bit discouraged as they looked at
the outside of the Spa House, the row of cottages and then
Greystones. Then Charlie looked up at the gateposts at the
entrance to Aunt Eliza's house and laughed.

'What a proper Charlie I am!' he said laughing. 'I've
looked at these stone statues so many times, but I've never
really noticed what they are! Look, you can just make out
that they're pelicans. That must be what we're looking for.'

'It's strange,' commented Toby, 'because Auntie told us that those carvings came from the old manor house—they don't really belong to Greystones.'

'Well, the manor was demolished in the twentieth century,' said Tilly, 'so Vi must have hidden the clue up there. I wonder how she did it?'

'That doesn't matter; what matters is that we find the right pelican,' answered Toby. 'I'll ask Aunt Eliza for a stepladder and we can see if one of them is loose. I hope the treasure is still there because it could have been lost when they were brought down here.'

A stepladder was duly found and brought to the gateway. The children felt nervous because they realized that the trail might go cold. Charlie climbed the ladder up to one of the pelicans while Toby held it firmly in case his friend wobbled. Charlie was feeling gently all around the pelican to see if it was loose when Alfie spoke up.

'She didn't finish the poem,' he said excitedly.

'What do you mean?' asked Poppy.

'The rhyme goes, "What a wonderful bird is the pelican, its beak holds more than its belly can"; so we have to look in the beak.'

The others told Alfie that he was 'well cool' to know that poem, and he flushed with pleasure. Being the youngest, he was often teased or told he wasn't old enough to know or do something, so he was pleased he had remembered the rhyme.

When Charlie looked carefully at the beak he saw there was a line running round it, showing a join, but it was covered in bits of dirt, old bird droppings and even bits of grass.

'Can one of you go and ask Aunt Eliza for a blunt knife?' he asked. Tilly went running off straight away. Within minutes she was back with the implement and Charlie inserted it and cleaned the join around the pelican's beak. Then he was able to prise it open. Although it had been closed for nearly 170 years, the beak sprang open. It had hinges at the back and inside was lined with lead! It was a secret hiding place and it was full of beautiful shells.

'We need a bag because there are so many here,' said Charlie, and this time Alfie went running indoors. Aunt Eliza came out with him, intrigued to know what the children had found.

'They're amazing!' declared Charlie, as he handed them down, a few at a time. 'Many must have come from foreign places,' he said. 'I know all the ones you get round here— I've got most of those in my collection.'

Once the cavity was cleared, Charlie looked for the piece of paper with the next clue, but much to their disappointment, there was nothing there.

'What do we do now?' asked Poppy.

'I think we all go up to the den, have the picnic lunch I've been making, and think,' remarked Aunt Eliza sensibly. 'Bring the shells: it could be that the clue is folded up inside one of the larger ones.'

Within minutes every crumb had been eaten and the children were looking at the shells, thinking that Aunt Eliza must be right; but again, they were disappointed as no clue was found.

'That must be the end of the treasure hunt, I suppose,' said Tilly, feeling sad. 'I must finish reading the diary—

perhaps there's some clue in it as to what happened to Mab in the end.'

'I've just had a thought,' said Toby. 'It might be daft, but why don't we look in the other pelican's beak, in case it has been left there?'

'First tidy up the picnic things and take them indoors, please,' said Aunt Eliza, 'and I'll get the stepladder out again. It's worth a try.'

This time Toby went up the ladder as it had been his idea. He had to scrape away all the debris from many years, just as Charlie had done, and then gently open the beak. There were shells inside this pelican, too! A few at a time they were handed down and put into another bag. Mab had truly had an amazing collection! No wonder she didn't want them to be burnt!

Right at the bottom of the beak was a large pink conch shell, inside which was tucked a piece of paper.

'We've found it!' shouted Poppy in delight.

'Take it carefully into the snug,' Aunt Eliza instructed them. 'As before, the paper will be very fragile by now, and again we'll probably need my magnifying glass to read the writing.'

Chapter fifteen

*I*n the snug Aunt Eliza slowly read out the clue. It was obviously the very last one:

My life is ending very fast,
So I have left the best till last.
St Ann will guard my treasure well—
Who will find it? I cannot tell.
But now my work on earth is done;
I hope the seekers have great fun.
No treasure's greater than this book,
But you must read it—not just look.

'It seems you have just one more treasure to find,' remarked Aunt Eliza. 'You have had fun, haven't you?'

'It looks like we have to search for the last thing at St Ann's Church,' stated Tilly. 'When can we do that?'

Before Aunt Eliza had a chance to answer, Tilly's mobile rang. Glancing at it she saw that it was their dad. That was unusual, as they always talked to him in the evening. A shiver went down her spine as she pressed the button to answer. Was everything OK with their mum?

'Hi, sweetie,' said her dad, 'are you all there, and Aunt Eliza too? If so, put the speaker on.'

Tilly pressed the loudspeaker button so that everyone could hear.

'Have you made any plans for tomorrow?' their dad asked. They all shouted 'No'.

'Then I have a treat for you all. I'm allowed to take Mum out for the day, to see how she copes. So I thought I'd bring her down to Nottington tomorrow. Will that be OK?'

Once again, they all shouted in unison, this time 'Yes!'

'Wonderful!' said Dad. 'We'll try to arrive about noon, then, after a light lunch, Mum can sit in her wheelchair by the river for a while before I drive her back to the hospital. She'll get tired very quickly but she's longing to see you.'

They chatted a little more, then Dad rang off.

Aunt Eliza smiled at the children. 'I guess we don't have to decide just now when we'll go to St Ann's to search for the last treasure. We need to plan for tomorrow. If you don't mind, Charlie and Poppy, I think it would be best if you went home now so that we can plan the day. Tilly, Toby and Alfie's mum will need as much rest and quiet as we can give her. Why don't we text you after lunch tomorrow, and if you're free you can come and play in the river.'

They nodded their agreement if their mother didn't have other plans.

'Now, children,' Aunt Eliza addressed Tilly, Toby and Alfie. 'What do you think your mum would like for lunch?'

Soon they were making plans. Tilly and Toby went on their bikes to the small supermarket on the Dorchester Road to get some smoked salmon to make their mum's favourite sandwiches.

That night in bed, after she had prayed to Jesus, thanking Him that her mum was getting better and for all the fun of the day, Tilly opened the diary to read some more:

'Dear Diary'—Tilly noticed that this was the very last entry and the writing wasn't as strong as before. She thought about Mab and felt sorry that she was becoming weaker and maybe was about to die. Then she looked at the page again:

Each day now I find it harder to breathe. I have the windows open as much as possible, but I'm not strong enough to stand up any more. I know that my life is coming to an end—I feel it inside me, but I also learn it from others. Yesterday Grandmother and Grandfather came from Yeovil on the train to see me. They were given permission to come into my room, and each held one of my hands. They had tears in their eyes and I knew they were saying goodbye. Today Papa told me that Grandmamma and Grandpapa, his parents, are coming to visit me. I love all my grandparents so much and feel so sorry that they are sad. I want them to know that I am just going home to Jesus a little bit before them. I know they love Him too, so they shouldn't be sad.

I have seen Hamish Sebastian several times now, for Papa carries me to the window and Mama holds him up for me to see. It does make me sad to think that I won't be here to see him sit up, crawl or learn to walk and talk—but maybe I'll see it all from heaven.

Cook and Vi also are sad when they come into my room— but I want them to behave as they always do: to make me laugh and to smile with me. I keep telling Vi that once I am gone, she must look for another job. She can read and write quite well now and has promised to go on practising and then to teach her brothers and sisters. She mustn't just go back to her work as a scullery maid—she could work in a shop or office or maybe be a nanny. She must be the best she can be—we don't know how long our lives will last, so we must always do our very best in every way.

My last treasure has been hidden—I kissed it goodbye, for it is so precious and I couldn't bear to think of it being burned. I have read it every day for as long as I could. I hope whoever finds it will do the same and have the joy from it that I have had. I said a prayer for them, too, whoever they are, and asked God to bless them. So now, goodbye to you, dear Diary, for you have been my friend and helped me through these days. Thank you.

Mabel Louisa Henderson, aged 11 years.

August 1850

Tilly thought about Mab and tried to feel what it must have been like to die in this very room after living for only eleven years. She thought about the final clue and treasure; she was pretty sure she knew what would be found, but she decided not to tell anyone.

It was a long time after putting out the light before Tilly fell asleep. She found herself sometimes thinking about Mab and sometimes thinking about her mum and longing to see her.

The next morning was bright and sunny, but not so warm. The children helped their great-aunt to prepare the food for lunch, which made the time pass quickly. Tilly paddled through the river to the meadow on the other side so

that she could pick some wild flowers to put on the table.
Her mum had always loved wild flowers. As she picked
buttercups, daisies and meadowsweet, the fragrance
seemed to sweep right down into her heart. She felt like
singing. Everything around her looked so bright and
beautiful. It smelt 'countrified' and fresh—and now her
mum was coming to see it all!

When the car drew up by the gates, excitement bubbled
out of all three children and they rushed through the
stone archway with the pelicans on top, ready to hug their
parents.

Aunt Eliza stood behind them looking at her beloved
nephew, David, and his wife, Alice, who looked frail as
he carried her from the car and put her gently into the
wheelchair. Her heart ached as she watched the excited
children. Life would not be easy as they looked after their
mother, but she knew that with God's help and all the love
they had, they would make it through.

Lunch was a huge success—even though the children
were worried when they saw how much help their mum
needed to eat and drink. She couldn't hold a knife or
fork and could barely speak. Afterwards they pushed the
wheelchair under the apple tree where it was shady. Heinz
sat at her feet and was incredibly well behaved, as if he
instinctively knew he mustn't jump up or bark. One by one
the children sat with her and held her hand, telling her
bits about the holiday.

When it was Tilly's turn, the thing she most wanted to
share was that she had given her life to Jesus and wanted
to be baptized when she was back home. Her mum smiled

broadly at her, with tears in her eyes, and squeezed Tilly's hand with the little strength she had. Tilly kissed her.

'I love you to the moon and back, Mum,' she said. 'And don't worry, I'll help look after you, and you will get better.'

Poppy and Charlie then arrived and were introduced, and all the children went down to the river to play while the grown-ups looked on. It was fun in the water, and they were given permission to use the canoe which was stored in the garage. All too soon it was time for their dad to drive Mum back to the hospital, but the day had been a great success and Dad promised to bring her again soon.

Chapter sixteen

After all the excitement of the day, Tilly felt overwhelmed. She could see that her great-aunt was tired, so she offered to make the spaghetti bolognese planned for dinner. She liked to cook, and even though it was hot and stuffy in the kitchen and she could see the boys outside splashing around in the river once more, she needed time to think.

The holidays were nearly over and before long they would leave Greystones and return to their semi-detached suburban house in Bristol. School would start again, with homework to do in the evenings, as well as her dancing classes, music and netball club. She was looking forward to seeing Faith and telling her all about the adventures of the summer, instead of just texting and making the occasional phone call as they had done through the holidays. Strangely, she hadn't missed her social media apps as she'd thought she would when she had first heard that her great-aunt had no Internet.

Chopping up the onions and frying them caused tears to spring like a fountain from Tilly's eyes—but it wasn't just the onions; seeing her beautiful, energetic mum looking weak and struggling even to say a few words was hurting her.

After they had eaten and cleared away the dishes, the boys went to feed the ducks. The little ducklings were very tame and growing rapidly. Tilly put Heinz on his lead and took him for a walk through the village. He was learning to walk to heel very well but had boundless energy for such a young puppy. At the end of the lane she reached a meadow filled with buttercups and daisies where she let Heinz off the lead and played ball with him. A lump came into her throat: how she would miss this village, her new friends Poppy, Charlie and their mum and dad, Heinz and, most of all, Aunt Eliza. Who would have thought that such a stiff and starchy old lady could be such fun? She was glad that they lived near enough to come back often! Maybe she and Faith could come and stay sometimes—she hoped so!

By the time Heinz's walk had ended and she was back at Greystones, the boys were getting ready for bed.

'Auntie,' she asked, 'it's still hot; would it be all right if I sat in the apple tree for a while before I go to bed?'

'Yes, Tilly, that's fine,' Aunt Eliza replied, 'but I'm a bit tired and want to head up to bed, so please don't stay out too long, and make sure you lock the back door when you come back in.'

Tilly had her shower, put on her pyjamas and grabbed her book which Aunt Eliza had lent to her: it was *Jo's Boys*. She'd read the first book in the series, *Little Women*, at school and liked it, so was pleased to read more about the March girls.

The old apple tree was easy to climb, and she could see why Mab had loved to sit in it. The leaves hid you from the world—you could see, but not be seen. There was a place where you could sit and lean back on a branch and feel really comfortable. It was still light, but Tilly had a little shoulder bag slung across her body containing her torch and phone, just in case Dad rang. Soon she was engrossed in the story of Jo starting a boys' school where they seemed to have as much fun as she and her brothers had been having here at Greystones.

The time passed quickly, and Tilly reached for her torch as the light faded. The leaves rustled gently, and she enjoyed the cool evening breeze. She wondered if she would hear the barn owl tonight—she had heard him from her bedroom several times during her stay in Nottington.

After a while Tilly heard a different noise—one coming from the river. She turned off her light and looked through the gloom—would she see the otters playing? Her eyes soon adjusted to the dark, and she saw that it wasn't otters but two men in a canoe. Something made her shiver—and she reached for her phone and took a picture. The men moored the canoe at the steps just below the kitchen door, and then they came through the gate and up into the garden, talking quietly.

'The lights are out,' the taller one said. 'I think the old biddy's gone to bed.'

'Look, there's the garage. That Alfa Romeo is worth a fortune! I've heard she has it kept in tip-top condition, so we should be able to start it and make a quick getaway. Shouldn't take me long to pick the lock. You open the drive gates, then get the canoe—we don't want to leave any evidence. And just in case of prying eyes, put on your balaclava for the time being.'

Tilly was scared—so scared that she began to tremble. What could she do? These men were about to steal Aunt Eliza's car! Then suddenly she felt calm, and it was as if a voice inside her was instructing her:

'Phone 999 and call the police. Speak quietly, but slowly and clearly; you are far enough away that you will not be heard.'

Tilly obeyed the 'voice'; somehow, she felt as if an angel was telling her what to do. She was able to give a clear message to the police and was told to stay where she was and take photos on her phone if possible.

Once she had made the phone call, the shorter, fatter of the two men came back down the steps to the river and picked up the canoe, carrying it back towards the garage. He made a bit of noise and Heinz started barking from his bed in the snug. The man stopped still and waited until the barking had stopped, then he continued as quietly and slowly as he could.

'Good,' thought Tilly, 'that gives the police a bit more time.'

Meanwhile, she was able to see that the garage doors were open and both men were inside. Soon, the shorter man came back out and began to carry the canoe into the garage.

As Tilly moved slightly to one side to see a little better, her book fell out of the tree. The noise of it crashing to the ground made the man stop and look round.

'Something's not right—a book's just fallen out of that tree,' he said quite loudly to the other man, who had just got the car engine ticking over.

'Open those gates quickly, get the canoe in and then have a quick look,' said the other man with a curse. 'We need to get out of here asap.'

'Don't be frightened,' the voice inside Tilly said, calming her. 'I am with you.'

She put her phone and torch in her bag and sat with her arms around her knees, too scared to move a muscle. But the next thing she knew, the short man was climbing the tree and pulling her down!

'It's a dratted kid!' he said, almost shouting this time, which made Heinz bark loudly. 'We'll have to take her with us and dump her somewhere on the way.'

Tilly was roughly manhandled towards the garage and thrown into the boot of the car—but, although she was terrified, she also, in a strange way, knew that God was with her. The car began to pull out of the garage and into the drive. It had to go slowly to manoeuvre round the sharp bend of the lane and out onto the road. As they drove, they could hear the sound of a police siren—music to Tilly's ears.

'What the . . . ? Someone's phoned the Bill! Must be that brat in the back,' shouted the taller man, as he put his foot down on the accelerator, pulled out in front of the police car and drove off at speed through the village.

The road was very narrow. He sped over the speed bumps and didn't see the sharp turn, but instead went straight on, crashing into the hedge, with the car landing upside down in the farmer's field.

The men managed to jump out and tried to make a run for it, but they were quickly overtaken by the police and apprehended.

In the boot, poor Tilly was dizzy, had bumped her head and couldn't escape.

'Scream for all you're worth!' the 'voice' told her. 'Let them know you're in here!'

Tilly screamed and screamed, and soon the officers in the back-up police car which had just arrived ran over and tried to right the car and get her out. It took them several attempts, and by this time a few neighbours had gathered to help. They pulled a terrified Tilly from the boot and carried her gently away from the car.

They had freed her just in the nick of time. Suddenly, a huge explosion set the car alight. The flames flew high up in the air, and the noise and smoke were terrifying. Tilly heard gentle voices talking to her, but then there was nothing at all. When she awoke, she was in the back of an ambulance, with Aunt Eliza holding her hand.

Chapter seventeen

*B*eing in the Accident and Emergency department at the hospital was a daunting experience for Tilly, who had never had to be treated in such a place before. It had the same smell of disinfectant she had noticed when visiting the hospital where her mum was, and it stung her nose and throat—maybe they had been inflamed by the smoke of the explosion. The machinery around her reminded her of visiting her mum too, and she tried to pull the oxygen mask off her face. All she wanted to do was to go home with Aunt Eliza, but the doctor said she had to stay in the County Hospital overnight to make sure she was well.

It seemed hours before she was taken to the Kingfisher Ward for children—that was a much nicer place to be. A nurse helped her into a bed and she began to feel very sleepy.

'Go home, Auntie,' she whispered in a croaky voice to Aunt Eliza. 'I'll be all right here. You get a taxi and get some sleep.' Tilly knew her great-aunt must be very tired, and she felt safe and less scared now that she was on the ward. 'Please don't tell Daddy until tomorrow— he's got enough to worry about. And please give Heinz a big hug. I'm sure they'll let me out tomorrow. I feel very sleepy now.'

'If you're sure, darling,' Aunt Eliza said, giving her a kiss. 'Goodnight, and God bless. I'll see you tomorrow as soon as they let me.'

Tilly slept soundly. She had a feeling that she must have been given an injection or a tablet, because she felt a great sense of peace and knew nothing more until the morning, when the nurses were helping other children in the ward to have their breakfast.

She was a bit confused to wake up in a strange place, but she soon remembered all the adventure of the night before. The nurse helped her shower and found her some clothes to wear which more or less fitted her—some shorts and a t-shirt; her pyjamas were ruined. Her bag was in the locker by her bed and she thought she could text Charlie and say she was fine, and that he could tell her brothers and ask Aunt Eliza to bring her jeans, t-shirt and underwear.

By the time Aunt Eliza arrived, the doctor had checked Tilly again and told her she could go home. A nice young policewoman also came and chatted to Tilly, making notes as Tilly told her exactly what had happened the night before. The police officer asked if she could borrow her phone for a little while and put the photos she had taken from the tree in the police records. 'I'll bring it back to your great-aunt's house this afternoon, because I need to chat to her as well,' she promised.

Tilly went back with Aunt Eliza in a taxi—a much nicer way to travel than in an ambulance. When she arrived back at Greystones she was licked all over by Heinz, and within minutes of her arrival her brothers, Charlie and Poppy rushed in.

Later, after they had all eaten lunch, the policewoman arrived, returning Tilly's phone and wanting to chat to Aunt Eliza about the car.

'I feel so angry with myself,' Aunt Eliza told the officer. 'I should have sold it years ago. It was just sentimentality and pride that made me keep it. But last night it almost caused Tilly's death—and I feel so guilty that she ended up in hospital.'

'You weren't to know what would happen, and no one blames you,' the police officer assured her. 'Was the car insured?'

'Come to think of it, it was. I somehow had a dream that one day I would drive it again, so I kept it insured—it was too old to need road tax. I must have the certificate upstairs in my bureau.'

'If I were you, I would put in a claim very soon—the story will be in the papers, so get a copy and keep it. I will also add my report should proof be needed as it will eventually be evidence in a police enquiry. It should be worth quite a sum—that is why the men went after it. They're in police custody, so you don't need to worry about them, either,' the policewoman added.

'Can I phone Dad and tell him about my adventure?' asked Tilly, once the police officer had left.

'Yes, dear, but I need to speak to him too. I don't know what he'll think of me. I shouldn't have let you stay out in the tree last night. I feel so guilty.'

'Auntie, you heard the policewoman: it's not your fault, and I'm fine. Dad won't be cross.'

Tilly chatted to her dad on the phone and David learnt the whole story. He was just thankful that his daughter was fine.

'Can I come down tomorrow?' he asked. 'I've taken a few days off work to get the house ready for you all to come home—and that includes your mum, though she'll need carers to come and help her each day. I promised to take you out mackerel fishing and I haven't done it yet. It would be fun. I need to see Auntie and make arrangements as well.'

The boys were excited at the prospect of mackerel fishing—and Dad said that Charlie and Poppy were welcome to join them as well.

It proved a lovely day—the sea was calm and blue, the sun was shining and there was a gentle breeze. The fish were biting, too, and they caught lots. That evening they had a barbeque on Chesil Beach: it was a night to remember. Even Aunt Eliza came and with the help of cushions was able to sit comfortably on the pebbles.

'This has been such an amazing holiday,' Toby commented, 'even though Mum hasn't been with us. I thought it would be horrible, and I grumbled a lot about having to come. Now Mum is getting better and we've made new friends, had adventures and loved being with you, Aunt Eliza.'

'I was dreading you all coming,' said their great-aunt, 'but you've shown me that life can still be fun, even when you're old like me. I feel like a new person, and your father has asked me if I will come back with you for a few weeks until your mother is settled into her new routine.

We thought that I could stay until half-term, then you could all come back with me for the week's holiday.'

'That's well cool!' shouted Alfie. 'Thanks, Dad. It's like we belong here as well as in Bristol!'

Their father drove home that evening thanking God for his lovely family, including his aunt, while the children made plans for the next day.

'We need to go to St Ann's and find the last piece of the treasure,' Toby said. 'We can't go home until we've got it all!'

The others agreed and decided they would walk up to Radipole the following morning.

It was drizzling when they left Nottington, but no one minded. It had been hot for so long that it felt good to let the rain fall on their faces and run down their bare legs.

The church was open as it normally was during daylight hours. It was cool and a little dark inside, and it took a few moments for their eyes to adjust.

'Where shall we begin to look? It could be anywhere in this old church,' said Poppy.

'Mum said there was a story about a secret passage which ran under the pulpit to the manor house,' Charlie told them. 'I wonder if Vi hid it in there?'

'If she did, then we've had it,' Poppy told them. 'Our teacher brought us here one day when we were learning about churches, and she told us that the secret tunnel had been sealed off some while ago for safety reasons. It was under the first step of the pulpit.'

'Come on—let's all start exploring!' said Toby in his best organizing voice. 'You go upstairs, Charlie, and see if there are any hiding places in the gallery; I'll do the same in the porch; Alfie and Poppy, you look outside, and Tilly, you explore the main part of the building.'

'I'm glad you're with me,' Poppy told Alfie, 'Miss Steele told us there's supposed to be a ghost in the churchyard!'

'Wow! That makes it so cool! Come on, let's look around. I'm not scared—I expect it's only a story, anyway.'

Tilly was sure she knew what the treasure would be— and remembered that the clue said St Ann would guard it. As she looked around the building, she looked for hiding places. It seemed a bit derelict behind the organ, but she saw nothing that made her hopeful.

There was a lovely stained-glass window of Hope, Faith and Charity and she took a photo to show Faith. The next window set her mind thinking: it was of St Ann. 'Maybe St Ann is actually guarding it,' she said to herself, looking at the stones under the windowsill. She began to prod them, and suddenly, with a grating sound, one stone began to move. She called out to the others and pushed the stone further to reveal a cavity. 'I think I've found the hiding place!' she exclaimed.

Charlie came hurtling down the old stairs, while Toby ran to the graveyard to call Alfie and Poppy. Tilly waited for them all to join her before she slid her hand into the cavity and pulled out an old, crumbly cardboard box. It fell to pieces in her hand, revealing, just as she had guessed, a black leather Bible.

Tilly was very excited, but the others looked a little disappointed by the find. The Bible was small and the print inside was tiny. However, on the flyleaf they could read the words:

To the finder of my last treasure:

The Bible has helped me through these difficult months—God has spoken to me through it and I have read it every day. It is the most precious thing I own. Treasure it for me and read it every day of your life—and God will bless you, too.

Mabel Louisa Henderson
Anno Domini 1850

Tilly looked at the others, tears in her eyes.

'Do you mind if I ask Aunt Eliza if I can keep it and do as Mab says?' she asked. 'I want to read it every day and make her treasure real in my life.'

They all nodded their agreement—Tilly deserved it.